[redacted]

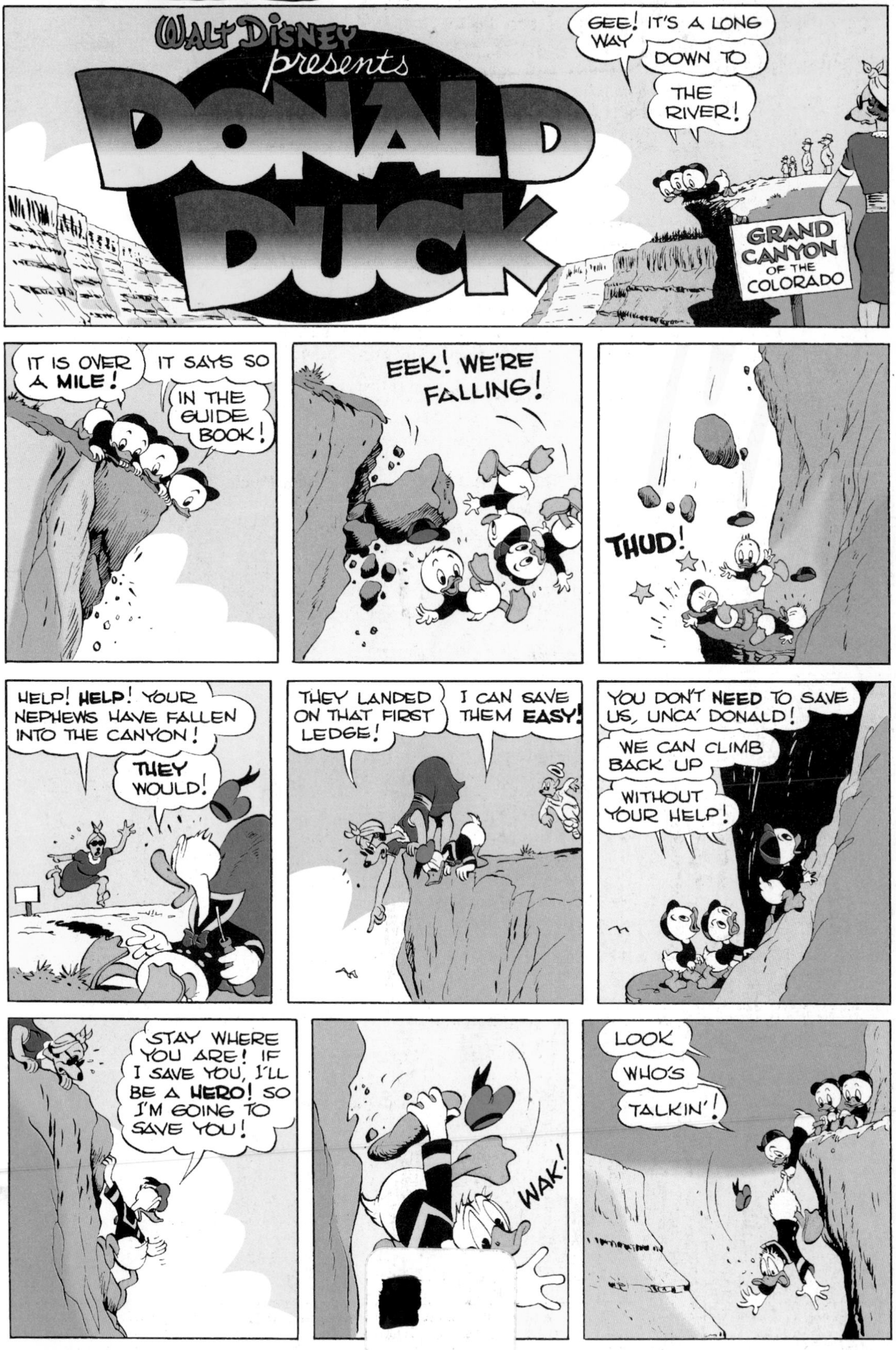
WALT DISNEY
presents
DONALD DUCK
GEE! IT'S A LONG WAY
DOWN TO
THE RIVER!
GRAND CANYON OF THE COLORADO
IT IS OVER A MILE!
IT SAYS SO
IN THE GUIDE BOOK!
EEK! WE'RE FALLING!
THUD!
HELP! HELP! YOUR NEPHEWS HAVE FALLEN INTO THE CANYON!
THEY WOULD!
THEY LANDED ON THAT FIRST LEDGE!
I CAN SAVE THEM EASY!
YOU DON'T NEED TO SAVE US, UNCA' DONALD!
WE CAN CLIMB BACK UP
WITHOUT YOUR HELP!
STAY WHERE YOU ARE! IF I SAVE YOU, I'LL BE A HERO! SO I'M GOING TO SAVE YOU!
WAK!
LOOK
WHO'S
TALKIN'!

[redacted]

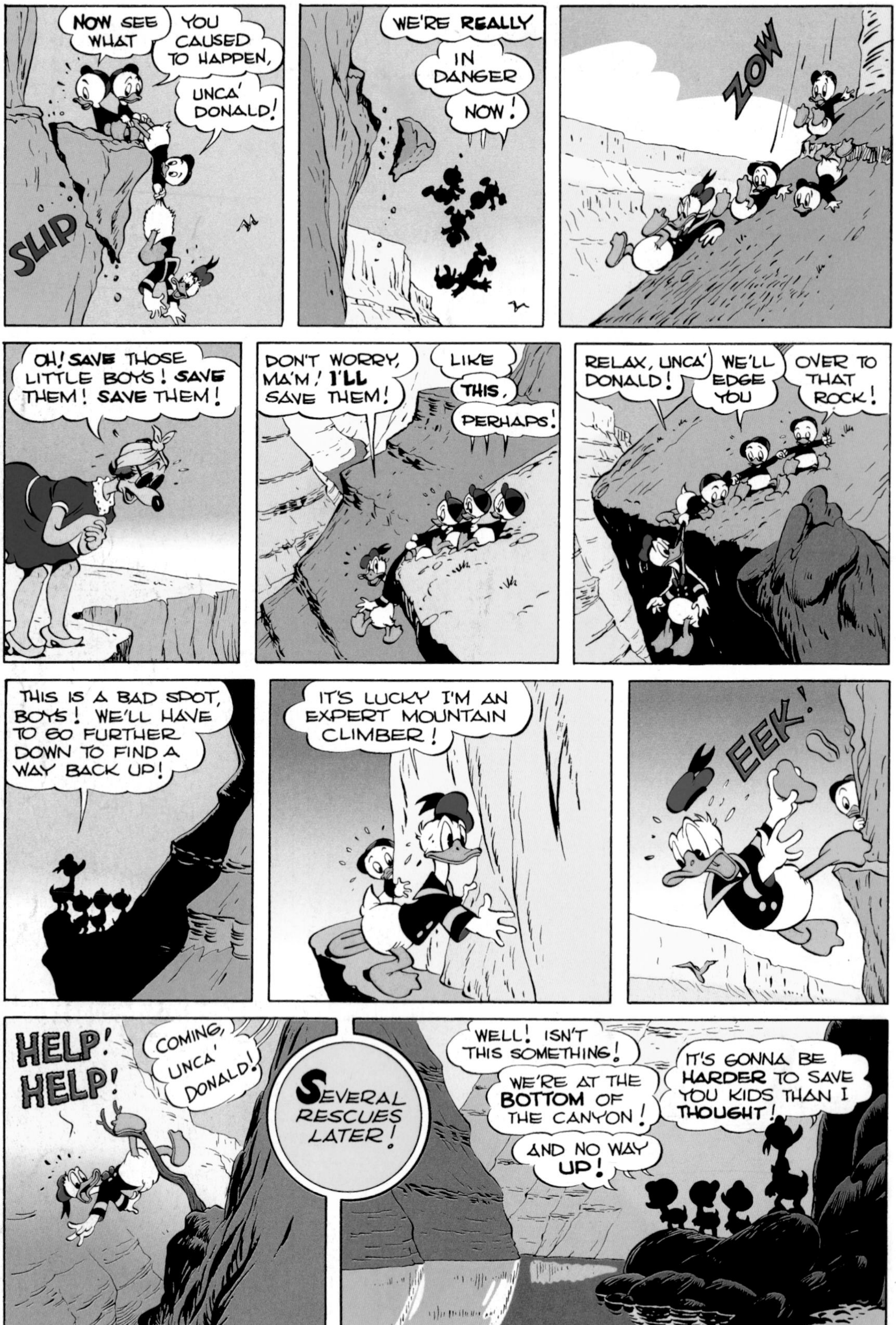
NOW SEE WHAT
YOU CAUSED TO HAPPEN,
UNCA' DONALD!
SLIP
WE'RE REALLY
IN DANGER
NOW!
ZOW
OH! SAVE THOSE LITTLE BOYS! SAVE THEM! SAVE THEM!
DON'T WORRY, MA'M! I'LL SAVE THEM!
LIKE
THIS,
PERHAPS!
RELAX, UNCA' DONALD!
WE'LL EDGE YOU
OVER TO THAT ROCK!
THIS IS A BAD SPOT, BOYS! WE'LL HAVE TO GO FURTHER DOWN TO FIND A WAY BACK UP!
IT'S LUCKY I'M AN EXPERT MOUNTAIN CLIMBER!
EEK!
HELP! HELP!
COMING, UNCA' DONALD!
SEVERAL RESCUES LATER!
WELL! ISN'T THIS SOMETHING!
WE'RE AT THE BOTTOM OF THE CANYON!
AND NO WAY UP!
IT'S GONNA BE HARDER TO SAVE YOU KIDS THAN I THOUGHT!

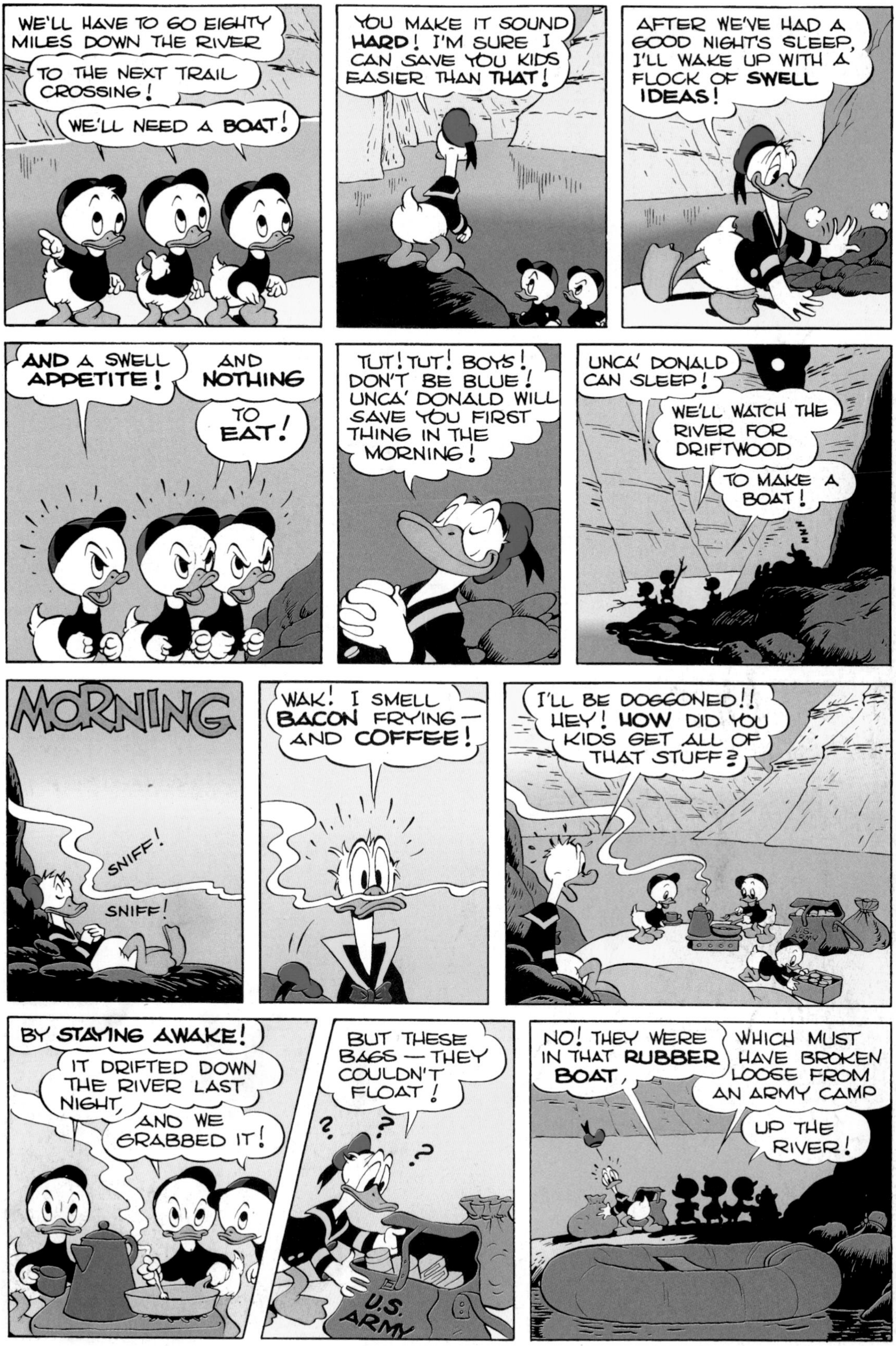
WE'LL HAVE TO GO EIGHTY MILES DOWN THE RIVER
TO THE NEXT TRAIL CROSSING!
WE'LL NEED A **BOAT**!
YOU MAKE IT SOUND **HARD**! I'M SURE I CAN SAVE YOU KIDS EASIER THAN **THAT**!
AFTER WE'VE HAD A GOOD NIGHT'S SLEEP, I'LL WAKE UP WITH A FLOCK OF **SWELL IDEAS**!
AND A SWELL **APPETITE**!
AND **NOTHING**
TO **EAT**!
TUT! TUT! BOYS! DON'T BE BLUE! UNCA' DONALD WILL SAVE YOU FIRST THING IN THE MORNING!
UNCA' DONALD CAN SLEEP!
WE'LL WATCH THE RIVER FOR DRIFTWOOD
TO MAKE A BOAT!
ZZZ
MORNING
SNIFF!
SNIFF!
WAK! I SMELL **BACON** FRYING — AND **COFFEE**!
I'LL BE DOGGONED!! HEY! **HOW** DID YOU KIDS GET ALL OF THAT STUFF?
U.S. ARMY
BY **STAYING AWAKE**!
IT DRIFTED DOWN THE RIVER LAST NIGHT,
AND WE GRABBED IT!
BUT THESE BAGS — THEY COULDN'T FLOAT!
? ? ?
U.S. ARMY
NO! THEY WERE IN THAT **RUBBER BOAT**,
WHICH MUST HAVE BROKEN LOOSE FROM AN ARMY CAMP
UP THE RIVER!

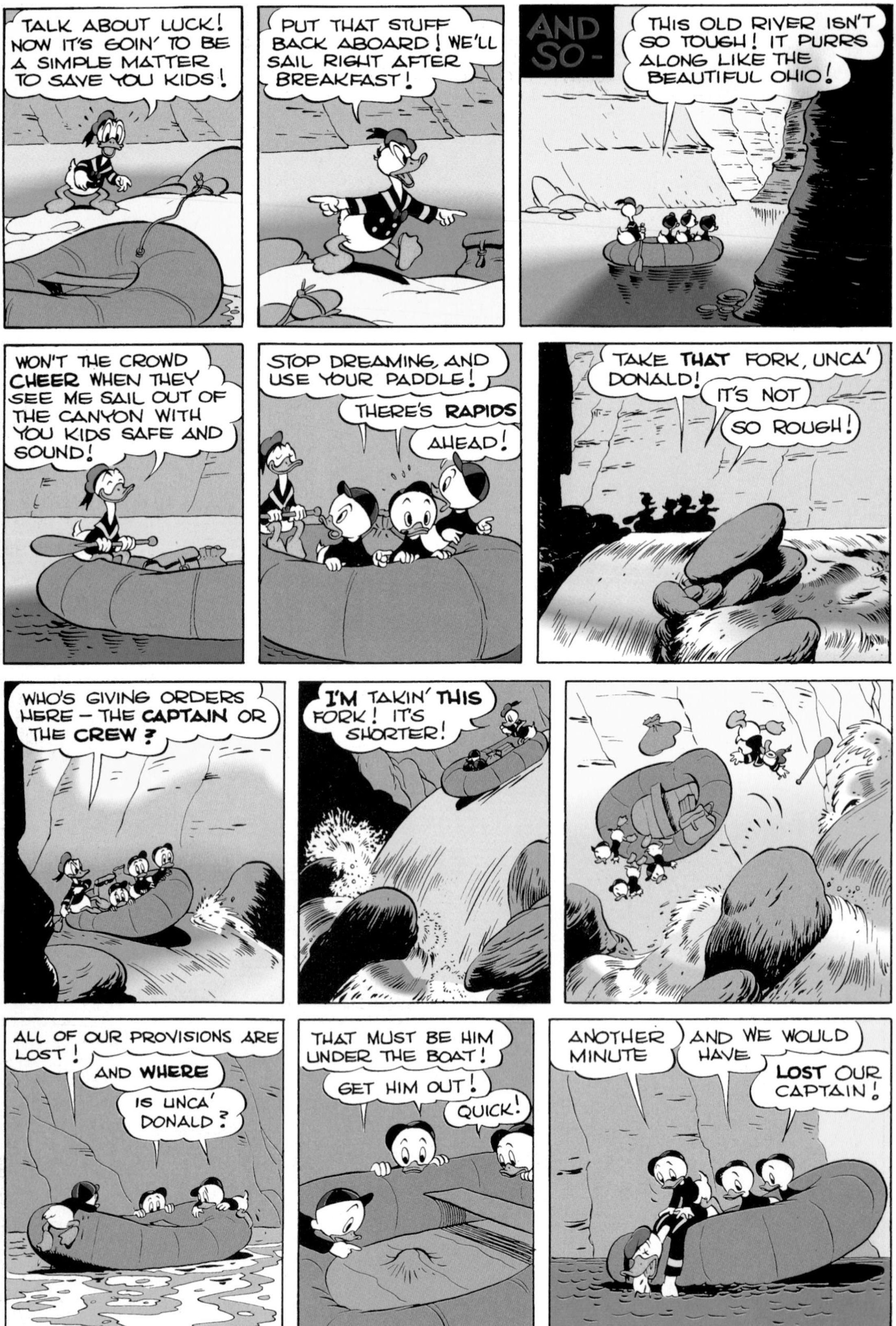
TALK ABOUT LUCK! NOW IT'S GOIN' TO BE A SIMPLE MATTER TO SAVE YOU KIDS!
PUT THAT STUFF BACK ABOARD! WE'LL SAIL RIGHT AFTER BREAKFAST!
AND SO-
THIS OLD RIVER ISN'T SO TOUGH! IT PURRS ALONG LIKE THE BEAUTIFUL OHIO!
WON'T THE CROWD CHEER WHEN THEY SEE ME SAIL OUT OF THE CANYON WITH YOU KIDS SAFE AND SOUND!
STOP DREAMING, AND USE YOUR PADDLE!
THERE'S RAPIDS
AHEAD!
TAKE THAT FORK, UNCA' DONALD!
IT'S NOT
SO ROUGH!
WHO'S GIVING ORDERS HERE – THE CAPTAIN OR THE CREW?
I'M TAKIN' THIS FORK! IT'S SHORTER!
ALL OF OUR PROVISIONS ARE LOST!
AND WHERE
IS UNCA' DONALD?
THAT MUST BE HIM UNDER THE BOAT!
GET HIM OUT!
QUICK!
ANOTHER MINUTE
AND WE WOULD HAVE
LOST OUR CAPTAIN!

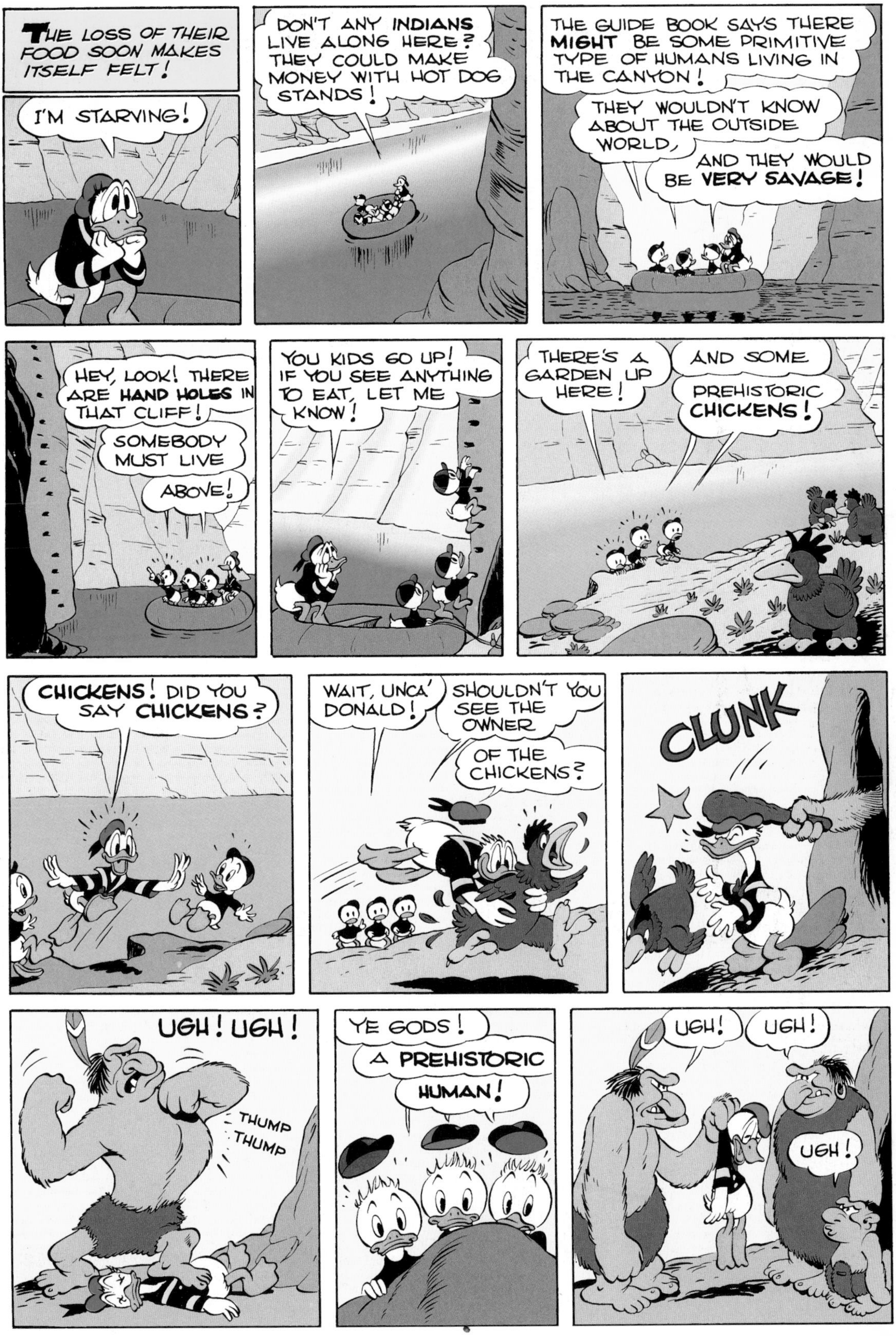

THE LOSS OF THEIR FOOD SOON MAKES ITSELF FELT!
I'M STARVING!
DON'T ANY INDIANS LIVE ALONG HERE? THEY COULD MAKE MONEY WITH HOT DOG STANDS!
THE GUIDE BOOK SAYS THERE MIGHT BE SOME PRIMITIVE TYPE OF HUMANS LIVING IN THE CANYON!
THEY WOULDN'T KNOW ABOUT THE OUTSIDE WORLD,
AND THEY WOULD BE VERY SAVAGE!
HEY, LOOK! THERE ARE HAND HOLES IN THAT CLIFF!
SOMEBODY MUST LIVE
ABOVE!
YOU KIDS GO UP! IF YOU SEE ANYTHING TO EAT, LET ME KNOW!
THERE'S A GARDEN UP HERE!
AND SOME
PREHISTORIC CHICKENS!
CHICKENS! DID YOU SAY CHICKENS?
WAIT, UNCA' DONALD!
SHOULDN'T YOU SEE THE OWNER
OF THE CHICKENS?
CLUNK
UGH! UGH!
THUMP
THUMP
YE GODS!
A PREHISTORIC
HUMAN!
UGH!
UGH!
UGH!

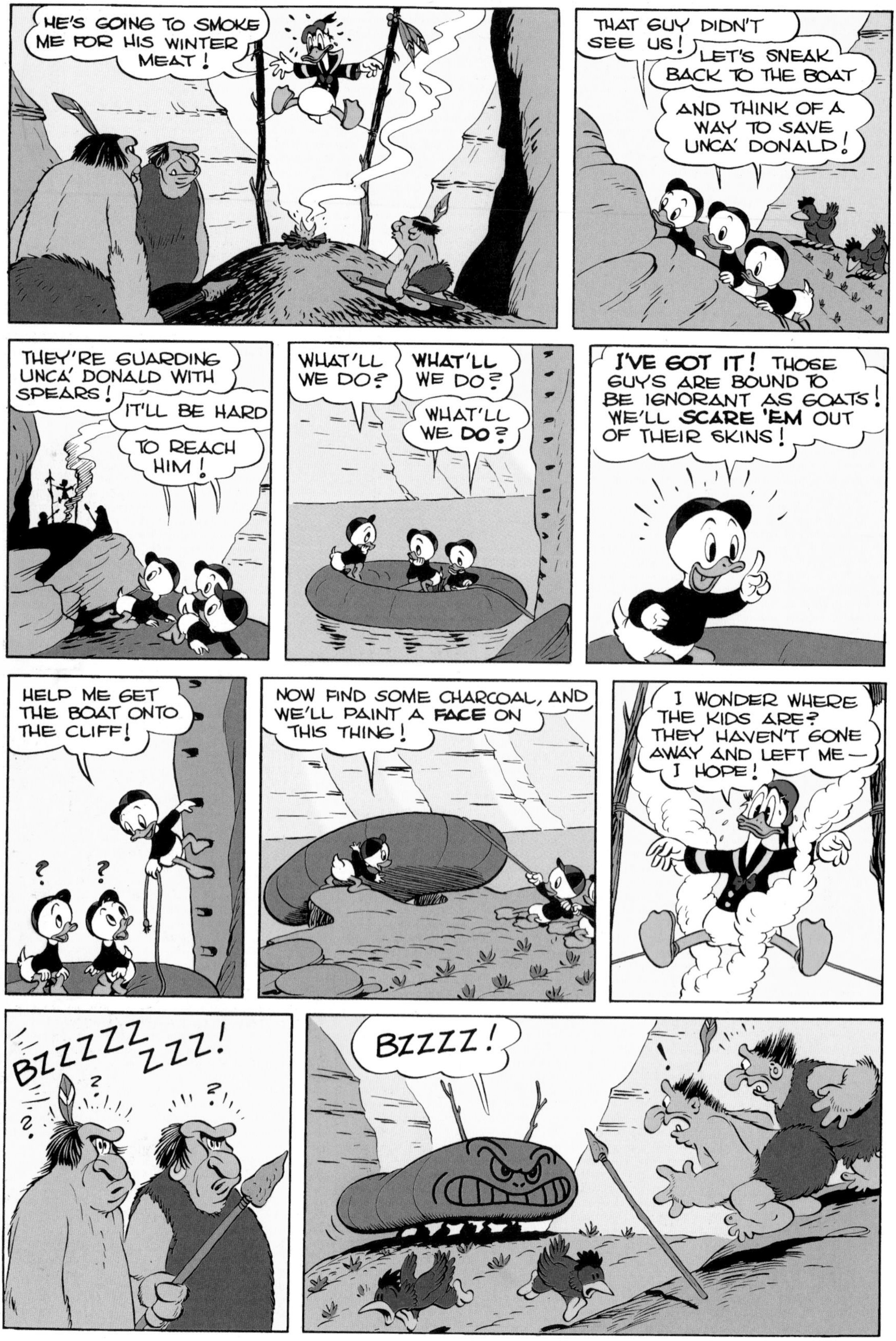
HE'S GOING TO SMOKE ME FOR HIS WINTER MEAT!
THAT GUY DIDN'T SEE US!
LET'S SNEAK BACK TO THE BOAT
AND THINK OF A WAY TO SAVE UNCA' DONALD!
THEY'RE GUARDING UNCA' DONALD WITH SPEARS!
IT'LL BE HARD
TO REACH HIM!
WHAT'LL WE DO?
WHAT'LL WE DO?
WHAT'LL WE DO?
I'VE GOT IT! THOSE GUYS ARE BOUND TO BE IGNORANT AS GOATS! WE'LL SCARE 'EM OUT OF THEIR SKINS!
HELP ME GET THE BOAT ONTO THE CLIFF!
?
?
NOW FIND SOME CHARCOAL, AND WE'LL PAINT A FACE ON THIS THING!
I WONDER WHERE THE KIDS ARE? THEY HAVEN'T GONE AWAY AND LEFT ME— I HOPE!
BZZZZZ ZZZ!
?
?
?
BZZZZ!
!

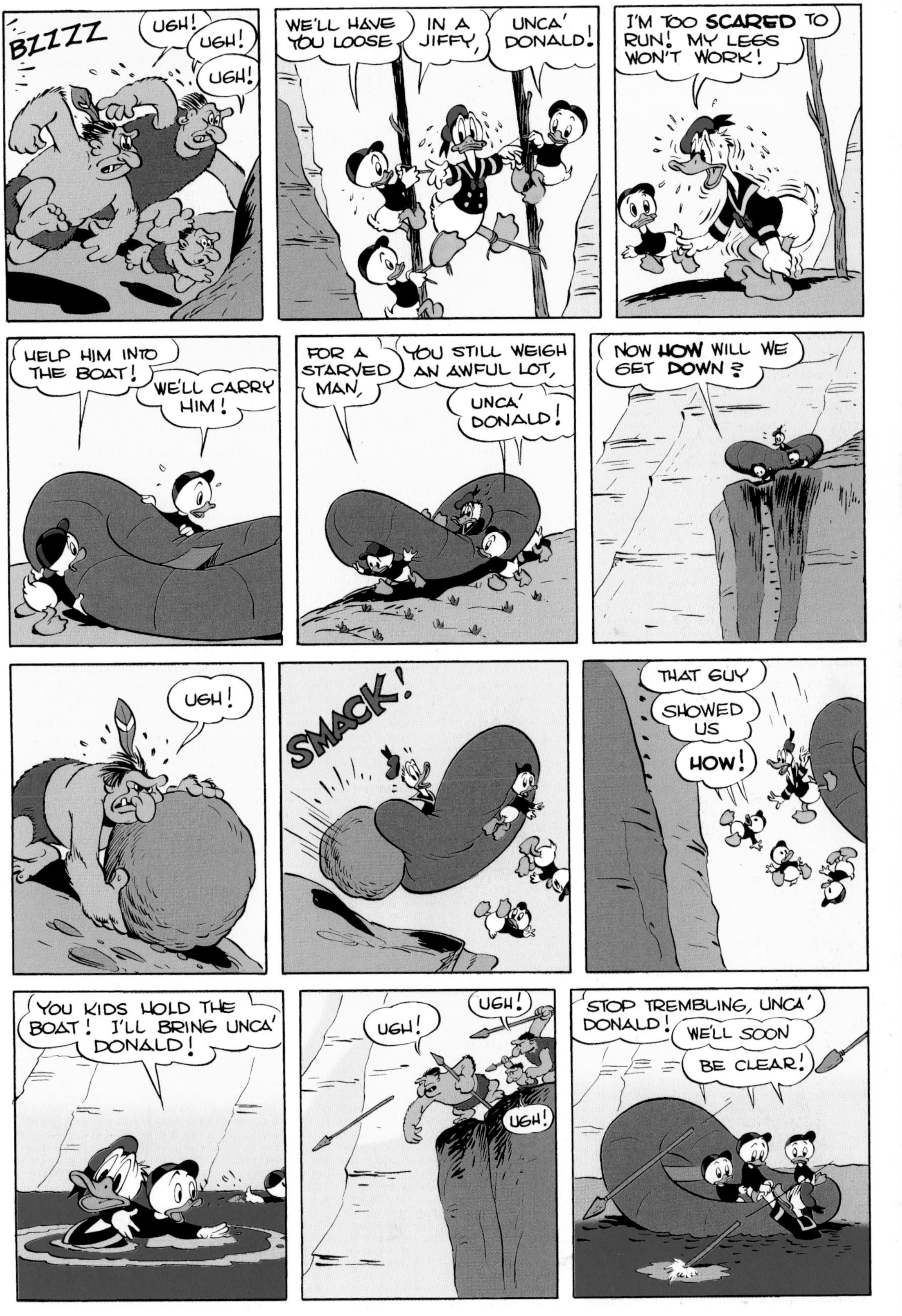
BZZZZ
UGH!
UGH!
UGH!
WE'LL HAVE YOU LOOSE
IN A JIFFY,
UNCA' DONALD!
I'M TOO SCARED TO RUN! MY LEGS WON'T WORK!
HELP HIM INTO THE BOAT!
WE'LL CARRY HIM!
FOR A STARVED MAN,
YOU STILL WEIGH AN AWFUL LOT,
UNCA' DONALD!
NOW HOW WILL WE GET DOWN?
UGH!
SMACK!
THAT GUY
SHOWED US
HOW!
YOU KIDS HOLD THE BOAT! I'LL BRING UNCA' DONALD!
UGH!
UGH!
UGH!
STOP TREMBLING, UNCA' DONALD!
WE'LL SOON
BE CLEAR!

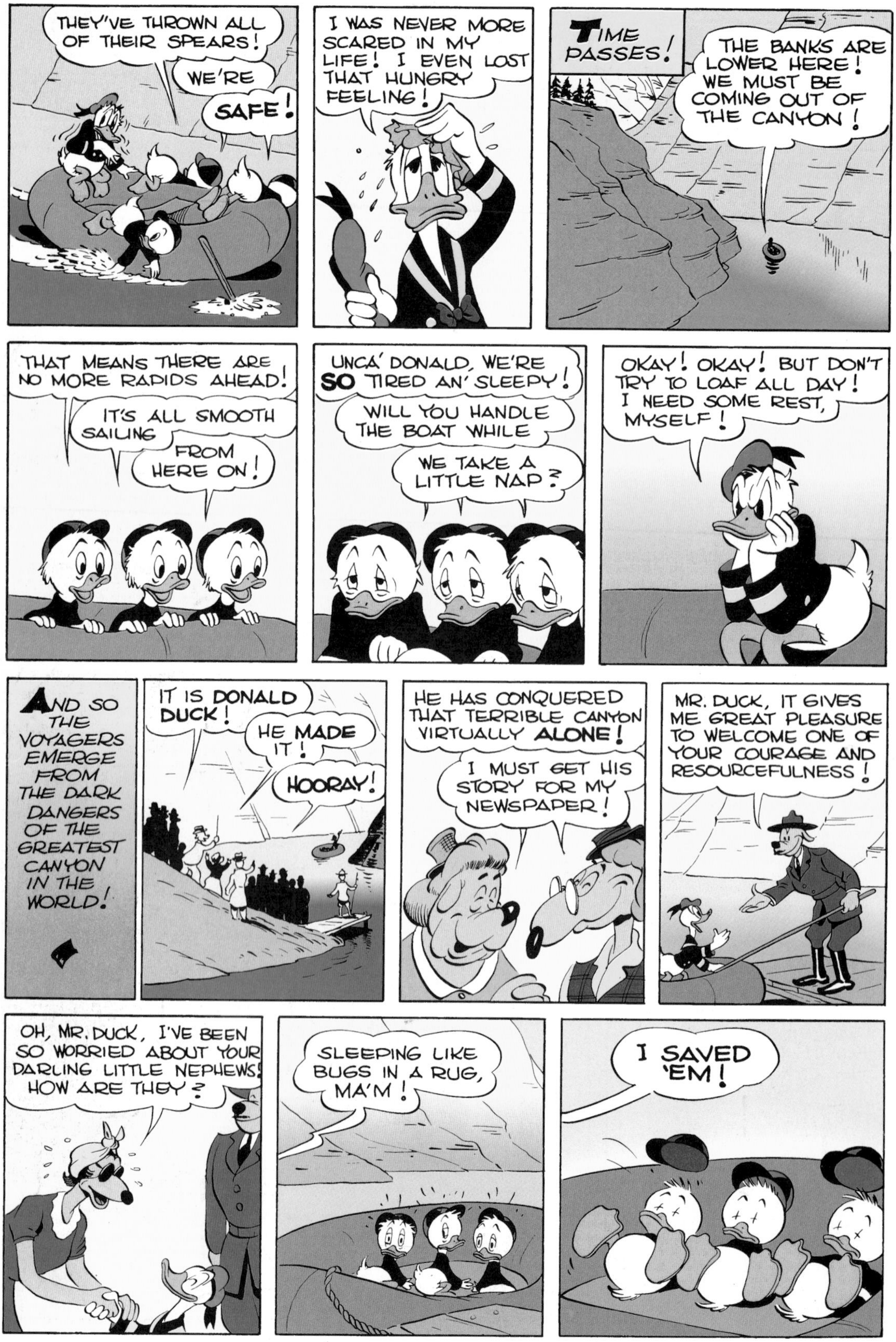
THEY'VE THROWN ALL OF THEIR SPEARS!
WE'RE
SAFE!
I WAS NEVER MORE SCARED IN MY LIFE! I EVEN LOST THAT HUNGRY FEELING!
TIME PASSES!
THE BANKS ARE LOWER HERE! WE MUST BE COMING OUT OF THE CANYON!
THAT MEANS THERE ARE NO MORE RAPIDS AHEAD!
IT'S ALL SMOOTH SAILING
FROM HERE ON!
UNCA' DONALD, WE'RE SO TIRED AN' SLEEPY!
WILL YOU HANDLE THE BOAT WHILE
WE TAKE A LITTLE NAP?
OKAY! OKAY! BUT DON'T TRY TO LOAF ALL DAY! I NEED SOME REST, MYSELF!
AND SO THE VOYAGERS EMERGE FROM THE DARK DANGERS OF THE GREATEST CANYON IN THE WORLD!
IT IS DONALD DUCK!
HE MADE IT!
HOORAY!
HE HAS CONQUERED THAT TERRIBLE CANYON VIRTUALLY ALONE!
I MUST GET HIS STORY FOR MY NEWSPAPER!
MR. DUCK, IT GIVES ME GREAT PLEASURE TO WELCOME ONE OF YOUR COURAGE AND RESOURCEFULNESS!
OH, MR. DUCK, I'VE BEEN SO WORRIED ABOUT YOUR DARLING LITTLE NEPHEWS! HOW ARE THEY?
SLEEPING LIKE BUGS IN A RUG, MA'M!
I SAVED 'EM!

Walt Disney's GOOFY in GREEN ICE CREAM AND A TRAMPOLINE

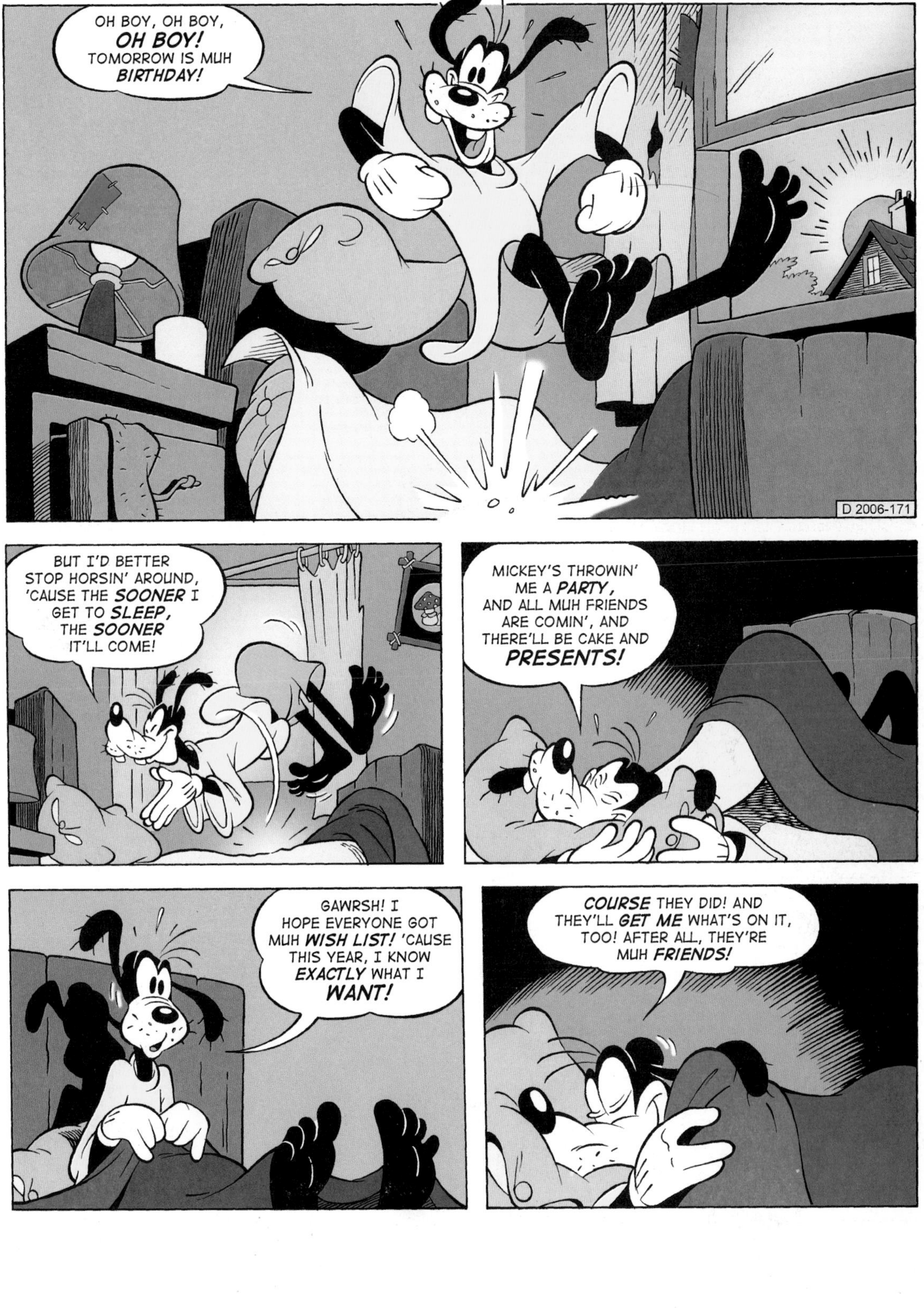

OH BOY, OH BOY, OH BOY! TOMORROW IS MUH BIRTHDAY!
D 2006-171
BUT I'D BETTER STOP HORSIN' AROUND, 'CAUSE THE SOONER I GET TO SLEEP, THE SOONER IT'LL COME!
MICKEY'S THROWIN' ME A PARTY, AND ALL MUH FRIENDS ARE COMIN', AND THERE'LL BE CAKE AND PRESENTS!
GAWRSH! I HOPE EVERYONE GOT MUH WISH LIST! 'CAUSE THIS YEAR, I KNOW EXACTLY WHAT I WANT!
COURSE THEY DID! AND THEY'LL GET ME WHAT'S ON IT, TOO! AFTER ALL, THEY'RE MUH FRIENDS!

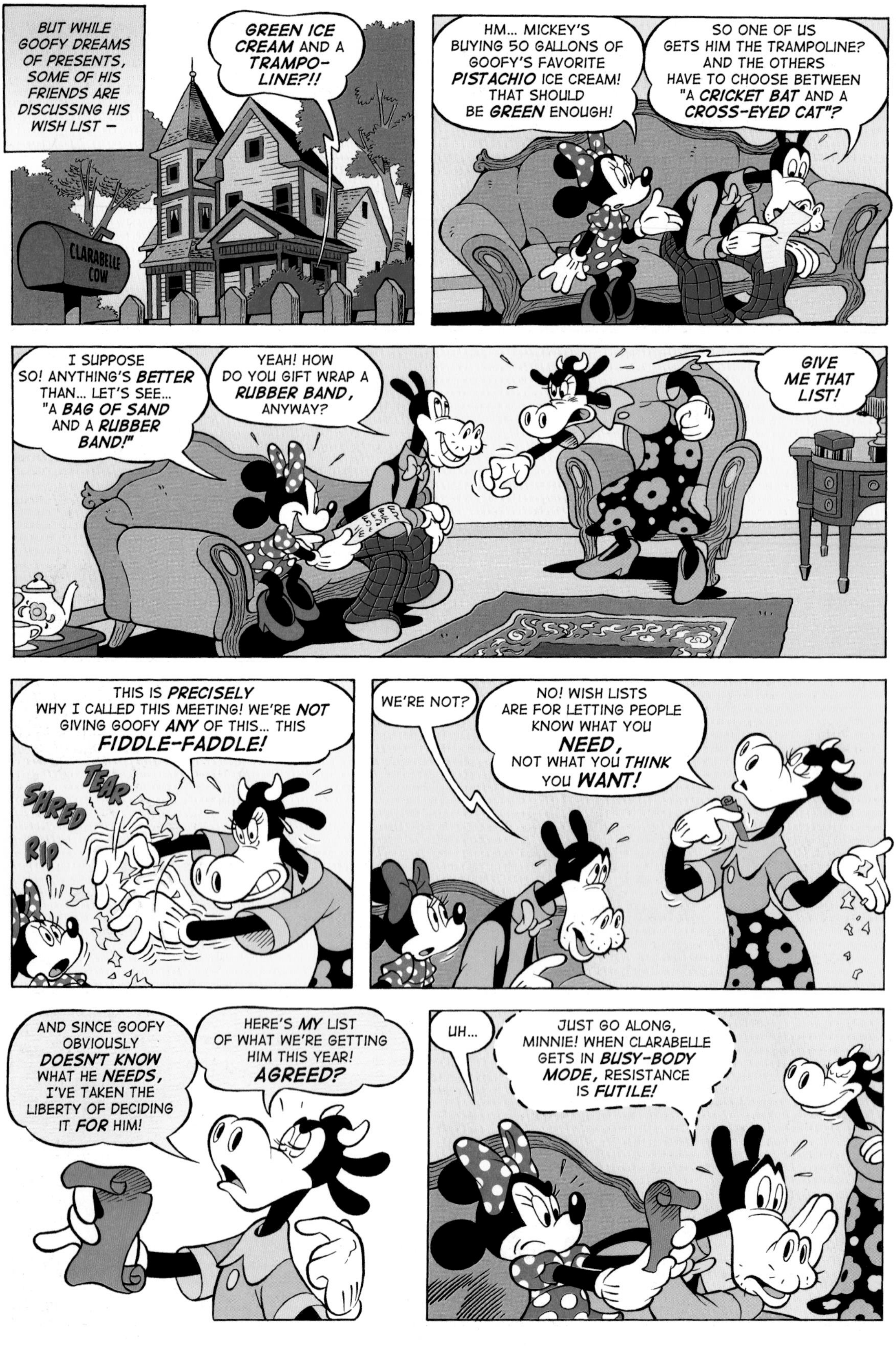

BUT WHILE GOOFY DREAMS OF PRESENTS, SOME OF HIS FRIENDS ARE DISCUSSING HIS WISH LIST –
GREEN ICE CREAM AND A TRAMPO-LINE?!!
CLARABELLE COW
HM... MICKEY'S BUYING 50 GALLONS OF GOOFY'S FAVORITE PISTACHIO ICE CREAM! THAT SHOULD BE GREEN ENOUGH!
SO ONE OF US GETS HIM THE TRAMPOLINE? AND THE OTHERS HAVE TO CHOOSE BETWEEN "A CRICKET BAT AND A CROSS-EYED CAT"?
I SUPPOSE SO! ANYTHING'S BETTER THAN... LET'S SEE... "A BAG OF SAND AND A RUBBER BAND!"
YEAH! HOW DO YOU GIFT WRAP A RUBBER BAND, ANYWAY?
GIVE ME THAT LIST!
THIS IS PRECISELY WHY I CALLED THIS MEETING! WE'RE NOT GIVING GOOFY ANY OF THIS... THIS FIDDLE-FADDLE!
TEAR
SHRED
RIP
WE'RE NOT?
NO! WISH LISTS ARE FOR LETTING PEOPLE KNOW WHAT YOU NEED, NOT WHAT YOU THINK YOU WANT!
AND SINCE GOOFY OBVIOUSLY DOESN'T KNOW WHAT HE NEEDS, I'VE TAKEN THE LIBERTY OF DECIDING IT FOR HIM!
HERE'S MY LIST OF WHAT WE'RE GETTING HIM THIS YEAR! AGREED?
UH...
JUST GO ALONG, MINNIE! WHEN CLARABELLE GETS IN BUSY-BODY MODE, RESISTANCE IS FUTILE!

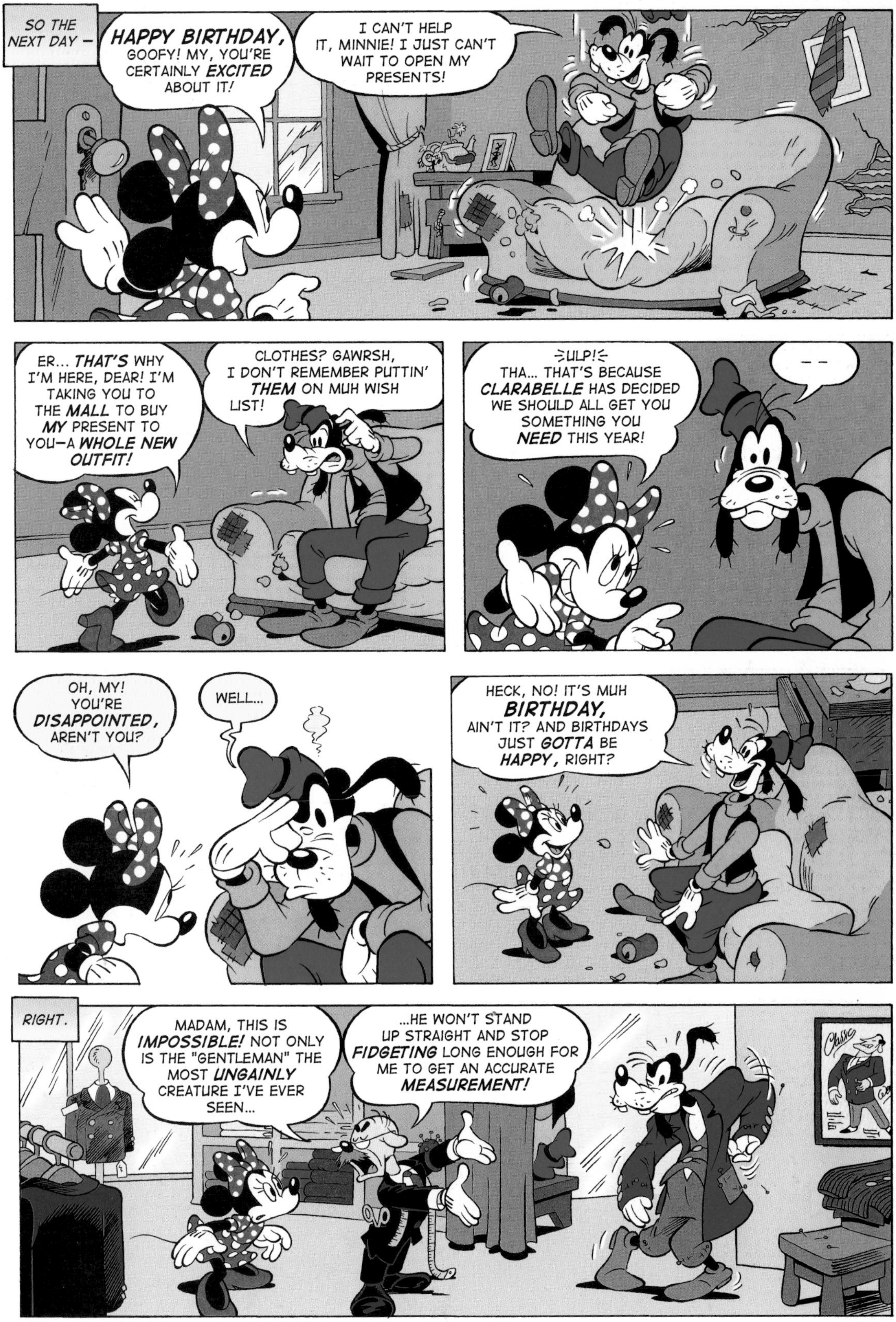
SO THE NEXT DAY —
HAPPY BIRTHDAY, GOOFY! MY, YOU'RE CERTAINLY EXCITED ABOUT IT!
I CAN'T HELP IT, MINNIE! I JUST CAN'T WAIT TO OPEN MY PRESENTS!
ER... THAT'S WHY I'M HERE, DEAR! I'M TAKING YOU TO THE MALL TO BUY MY PRESENT TO YOU—A WHOLE NEW OUTFIT!
CLOTHES? GAWRSH, I DON'T REMEMBER PUTTIN' THEM ON MUH WISH LIST!
GULP!
THA... THAT'S BECAUSE CLARABELLE HAS DECIDED WE SHOULD ALL GET YOU SOMETHING YOU NEED THIS YEAR!
— —
OH, MY! YOU'RE DISAPPOINTED, AREN'T YOU?
WELL...
HECK, NO! IT'S MUH BIRTHDAY, AIN'T IT? AND BIRTHDAYS JUST GOTTA BE HAPPY, RIGHT?
RIGHT.
MADAM, THIS IS IMPOSSIBLE! NOT ONLY IS THE "GENTLEMAN" THE MOST UNGAINLY CREATURE I'VE EVER SEEN...
...HE WON'T STAND UP STRAIGHT AND STOP FIDGETING LONG ENOUGH FOR ME TO GET AN ACCURATE MEASUREMENT!
Classic

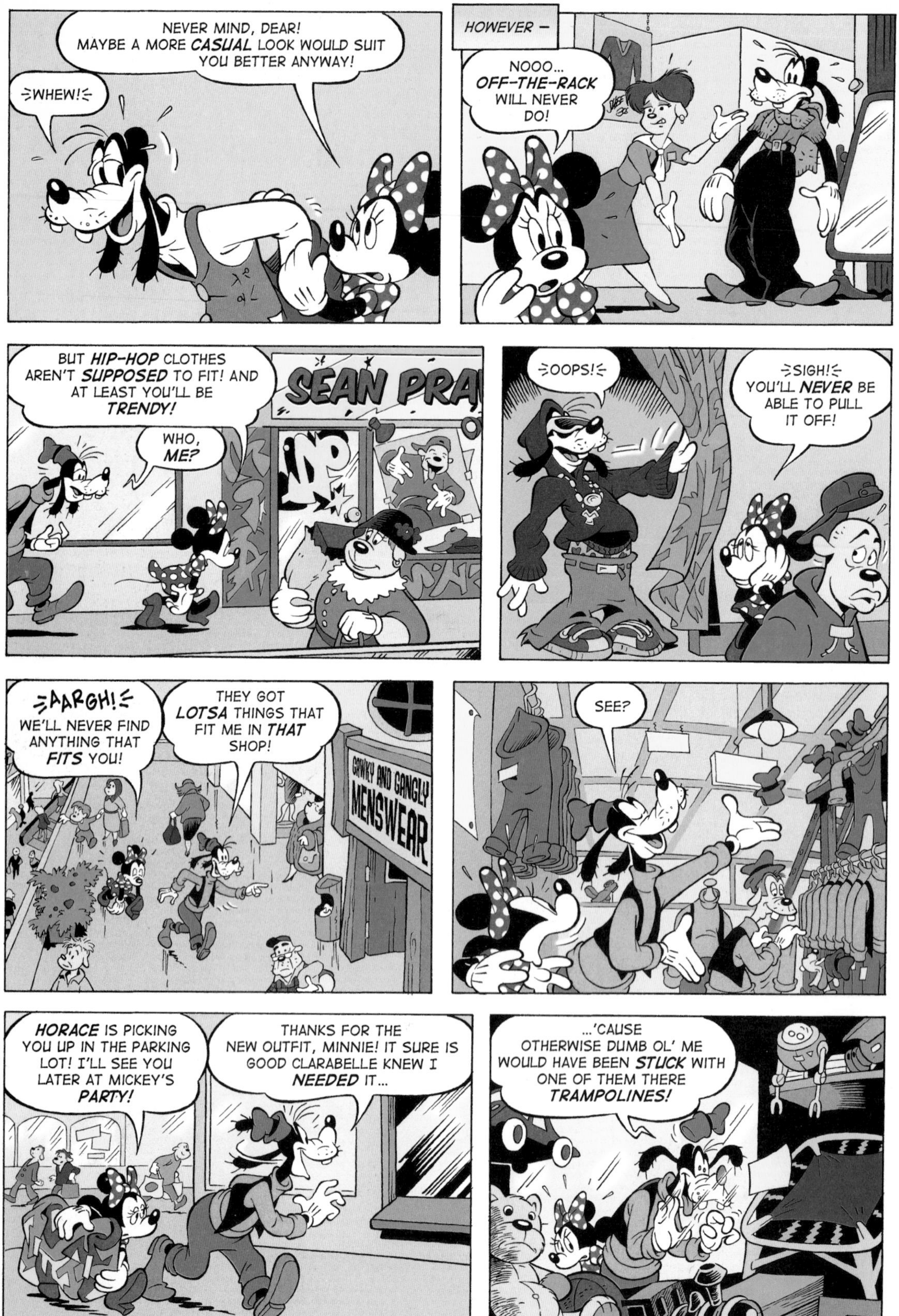
NEVER MIND, DEAR! MAYBE A MORE CASUAL LOOK WOULD SUIT YOU BETTER ANYWAY!
WHEW!
HOWEVER —
NOOO... OFF-THE-RACK WILL NEVER DO!
BUT HIP-HOP CLOTHES AREN'T SUPPOSED TO FIT! AND AT LEAST YOU'LL BE TRENDY!
WHO, ME?
SEAN PRA
OOPS!
SIGH! YOU'LL NEVER BE ABLE TO PULL IT OFF!
AARGH! WE'LL NEVER FIND ANYTHING THAT FITS YOU!
THEY GOT LOTSA THINGS THAT FIT ME IN THAT SHOP!
GAWKY AND GANGLY MENSWEAR
SEE?
HORACE IS PICKING YOU UP IN THE PARKING LOT! I'LL SEE YOU LATER AT MICKEY'S PARTY!
THANKS FOR THE NEW OUTFIT, MINNIE! IT SURE IS GOOD CLARABELLE KNEW I NEEDED IT...
...'CAUSE OTHERWISE DUMB OL' ME WOULD HAVE BEEN STUCK WITH ONE OF THEM THERE TRAMPOLINES!

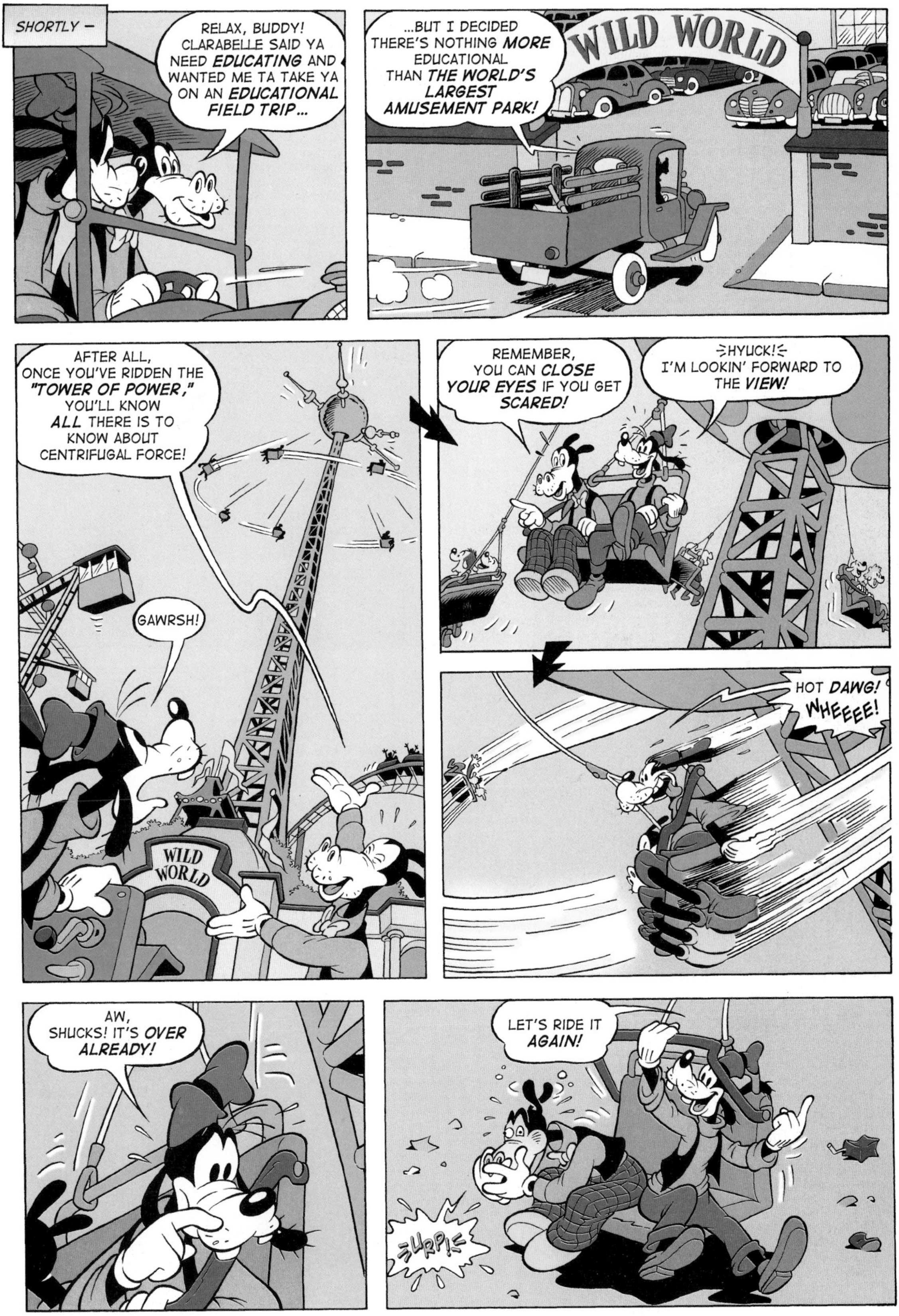
SHORTLY –
RELAX, BUDDY! CLARABELLE SAID YA NEED EDUCATING AND WANTED ME TA TAKE YA ON AN EDUCATIONAL FIELD TRIP...
...BUT I DECIDED THERE'S NOTHING MORE EDUCATIONAL THAN THE WORLD'S LARGEST AMUSEMENT PARK!
WILD WORLD
AFTER ALL, ONCE YOU'VE RIDDEN THE "TOWER OF POWER," YOU'LL KNOW ALL THERE IS TO KNOW ABOUT CENTRIFUGAL FORCE!
GAWRSH!
WILD WORLD
REMEMBER, YOU CAN CLOSE YOUR EYES IF YOU GET SCARED!
HYUCK! I'M LOOKIN' FORWARD TO THE VIEW!
HOT DAWG! WHEEEE!
AW, SHUCKS! IT'S OVER ALREADY!
LET'S RIDE IT AGAIN!
URP!

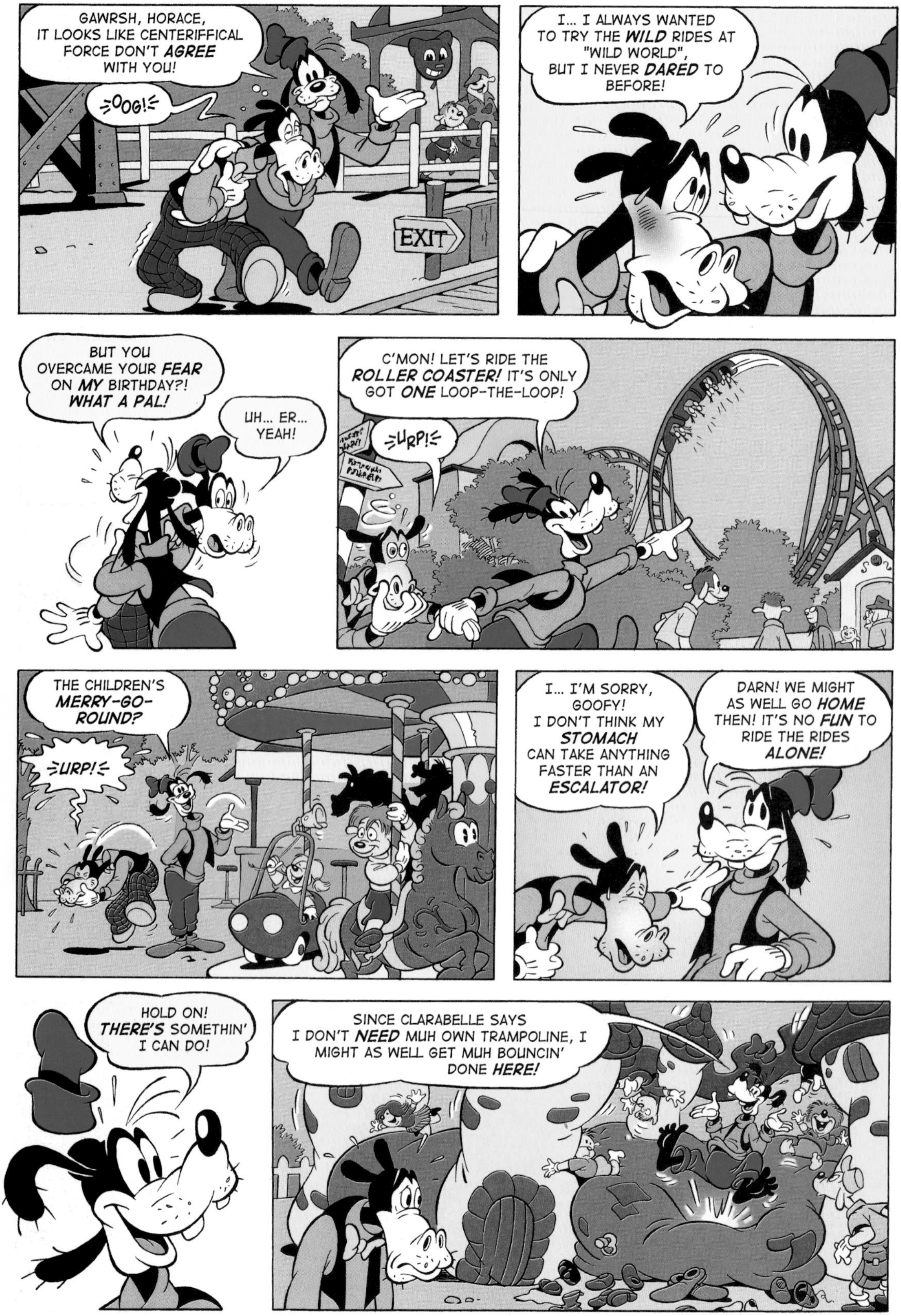
GAWRSH, HORACE, IT LOOKS LIKE CENTERIFFICAL FORCE DON'T AGREE WITH YOU!
OOG!
EXIT
I... I ALWAYS WANTED TO TRY THE WILD RIDES AT "WILD WORLD", BUT I NEVER DARED TO BEFORE!
BUT YOU OVERCAME YOUR FEAR ON MY BIRTHDAY?! WHAT A PAL!
UH... ER... YEAH!
C'MON! LET'S RIDE THE ROLLER COASTER! IT'S ONLY GOT ONE LOOP-THE-LOOP!
URP!
THE CHILDREN'S MERRY-GO-ROUND?
URP!
I... I'M SORRY, GOOFY! I DON'T THINK MY STOMACH CAN TAKE ANYTHING FASTER THAN AN ESCALATOR!
DARN! WE MIGHT AS WELL GO HOME THEN! IT'S NO FUN TO RIDE THE RIDES ALONE!
HOLD ON! THERE'S SOMETHIN' I CAN DO!
SINCE CLARABELLE SAYS I DON'T NEED MUH OWN TRAMPOLINE, I MIGHT AS WELL GET MUH BOUNCIN' DONE HERE!

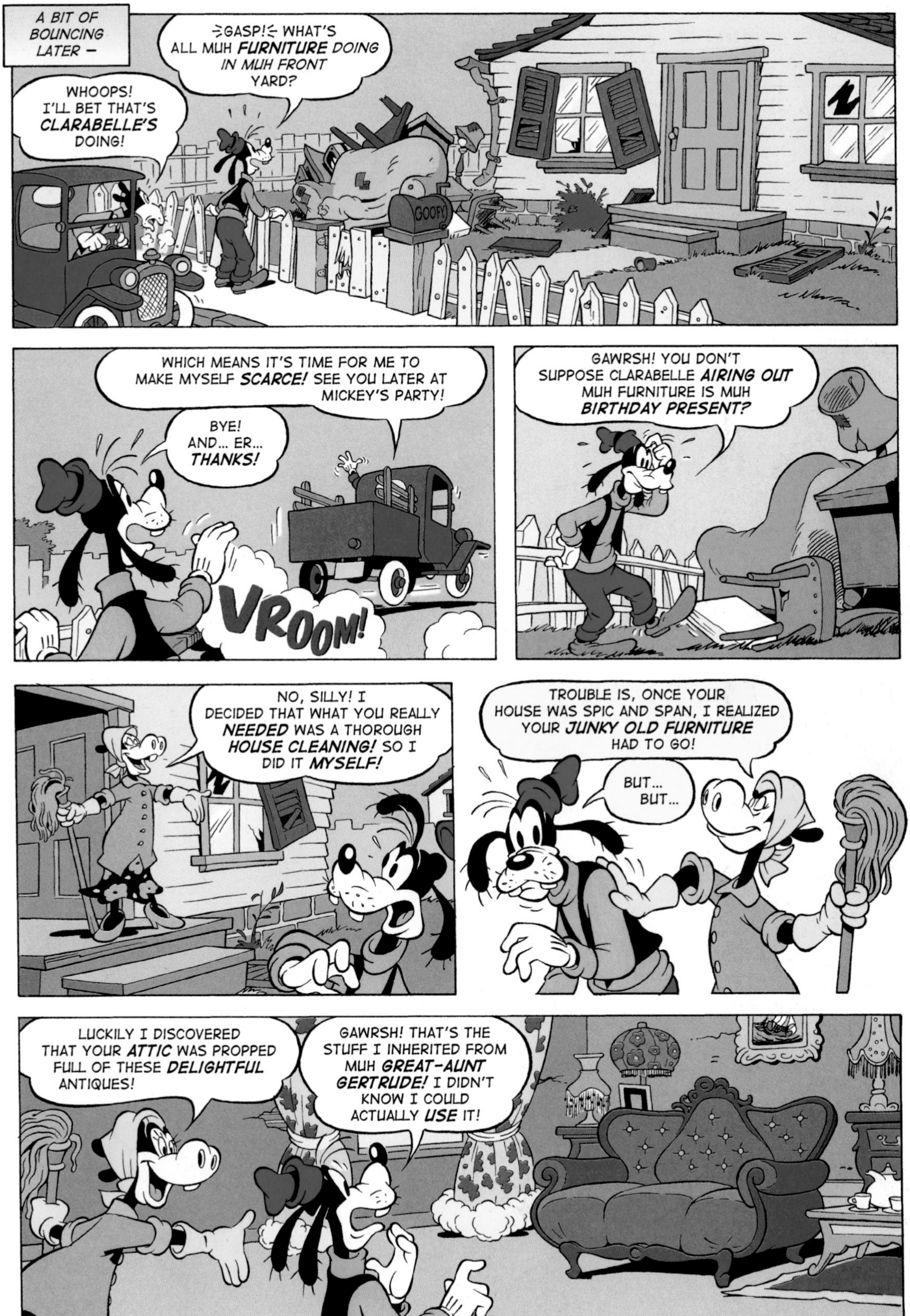
A BIT OF BOUNCING LATER –
WHOOPS! I'LL BET THAT'S CLARABELLE'S DOING!
⋛GASP!⋚ WHAT'S ALL MUH FURNITURE DOING IN MUH FRONT YARD?
GOOFY
WHICH MEANS IT'S TIME FOR ME TO MAKE MYSELF SCARCE! SEE YOU LATER AT MICKEY'S PARTY!
BYE! AND... ER... THANKS!
VROOM!
GAWRSH! YOU DON'T SUPPOSE CLARABELLE AIRING OUT MUH FURNITURE IS MUH BIRTHDAY PRESENT?
NO, SILLY! I DECIDED THAT WHAT YOU REALLY NEEDED WAS A THOROUGH HOUSE CLEANING! SO I DID IT MYSELF!
TROUBLE IS, ONCE YOUR HOUSE WAS SPIC AND SPAN, I REALIZED YOUR JUNKY OLD FURNITURE HAD TO GO!
BUT... BUT...
LUCKILY I DISCOVERED THAT YOUR ATTIC WAS PROPPED FULL OF THESE DELIGHTFUL ANTIQUES!
GAWRSH! THAT'S THE STUFF I INHERITED FROM MUH GREAT-AUNT GERTRUDE! I DIDN'T KNOW I COULD ACTUALLY USE IT!

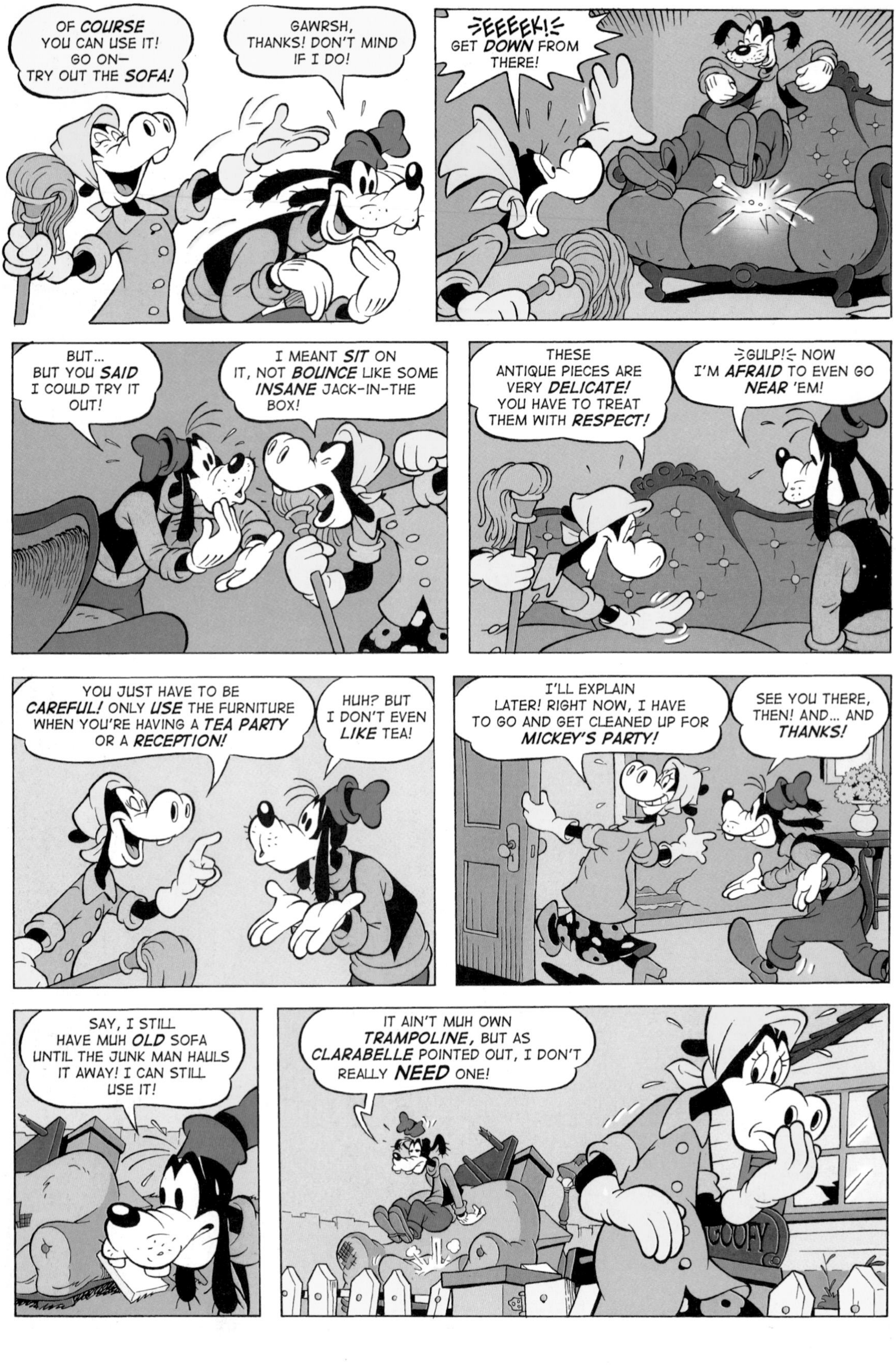
OF COURSE YOU CAN USE IT! GO ON— TRY OUT THE SOFA!
GAWRSH, THANKS! DON'T MIND IF I DO!
EEEEK! GET DOWN FROM THERE!
BUT... BUT YOU SAID I COULD TRY IT OUT!
I MEANT SIT ON IT, NOT BOUNCE LIKE SOME INSANE JACK-IN-THE BOX!
THESE ANTIQUE PIECES ARE VERY DELICATE! YOU HAVE TO TREAT THEM WITH RESPECT!
GULP! NOW I'M AFRAID TO EVEN GO NEAR 'EM!
YOU JUST HAVE TO BE CAREFUL! ONLY USE THE FURNITURE WHEN YOU'RE HAVING A TEA PARTY OR A RECEPTION!
HUH? BUT I DON'T EVEN LIKE TEA!
I'LL EXPLAIN LATER! RIGHT NOW, I HAVE TO GO AND GET CLEANED UP FOR MICKEY'S PARTY!
SEE YOU THERE, THEN! AND... AND THANKS!
SAY, I STILL HAVE MUH OLD SOFA UNTIL THE JUNK MAN HAULS IT AWAY! I CAN STILL USE IT!
IT AIN'T MUH OWN TRAMPOLINE, BUT AS CLARABELLE POINTED OUT, I DON'T REALLY NEED ONE!
GOOFY

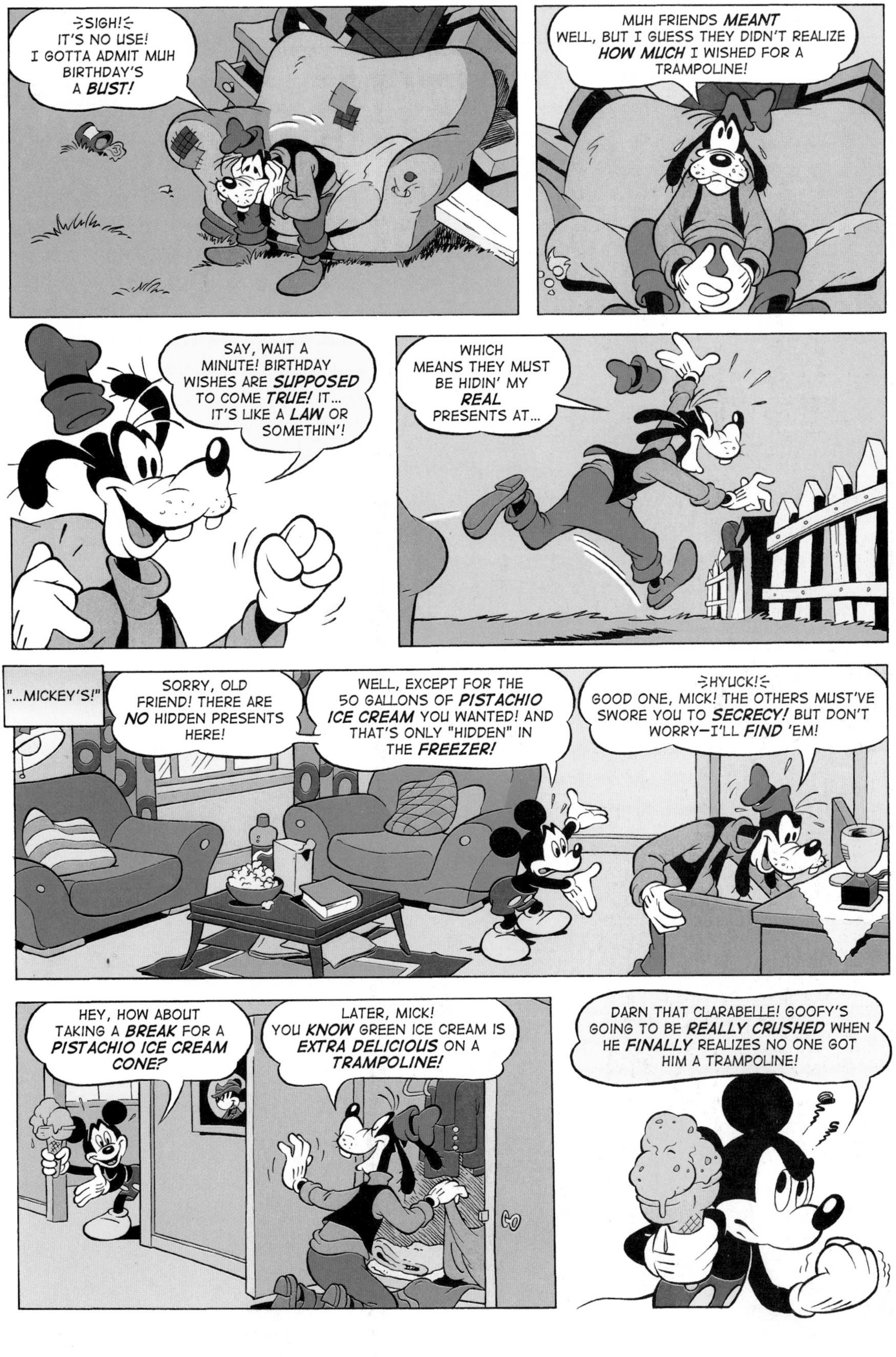

SIGH!
IT'S NO USE! I GOTTA ADMIT MUH BIRTHDAY'S A **BUST!**
MUH FRIENDS **MEANT** WELL, BUT I GUESS THEY DIDN'T REALIZE **HOW MUCH** I WISHED FOR A TRAMPOLINE!
SAY, WAIT A MINUTE! BIRTHDAY WISHES ARE **SUPPOSED** TO COME **TRUE!** IT... IT'S LIKE A **LAW** OR SOMETHIN'!
WHICH MEANS THEY MUST BE HIDIN' MY **REAL** PRESENTS AT...
"...MICKEY'S!"
SORRY, OLD FRIEND! THERE ARE **NO** HIDDEN PRESENTS HERE!
WELL, EXCEPT FOR THE 50 GALLONS OF **PISTACHIO ICE CREAM** YOU WANTED! AND THAT'S ONLY "HIDDEN" IN THE **FREEZER!**
HYUCK!
GOOD ONE, MICK! THE OTHERS MUST'VE SWORE YOU TO **SECRECY!** BUT DON'T WORRY—I'LL **FIND** 'EM!
HEY, HOW ABOUT TAKING A **BREAK** FOR A **PISTACHIO ICE CREAM CONE?**
LATER, MICK! YOU **KNOW** GREEN ICE CREAM IS **EXTRA DELICIOUS** ON A **TRAMPOLINE!**
DARN THAT CLARABELLE! GOOFY'S GOING TO BE **REALLY CRUSHED** WHEN HE **FINALLY** REALIZES NO ONE GOT HIM A TRAMPOLINE!

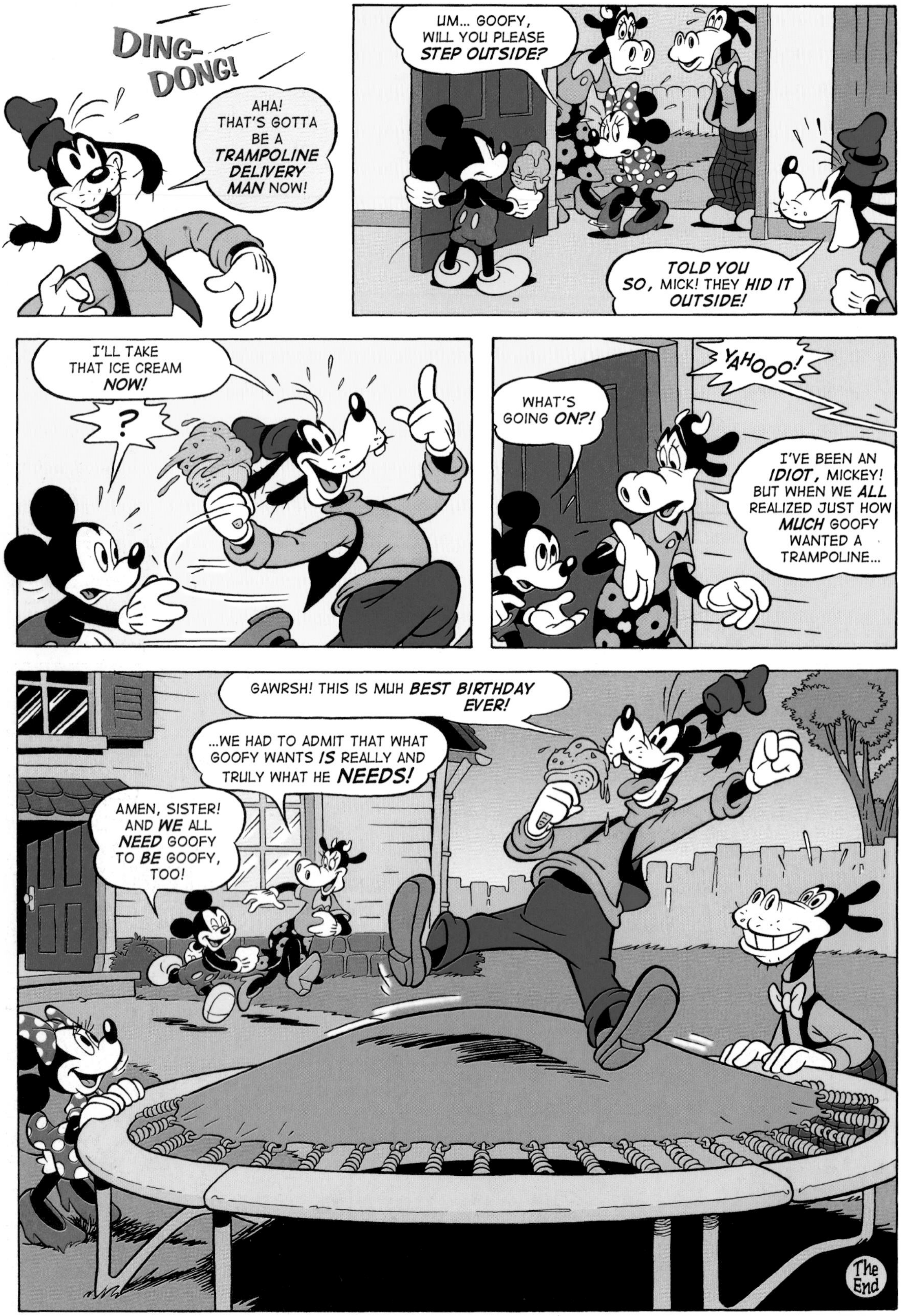
DING-DONG!
AHA! THAT'S GOTTA BE A TRAMPOLINE DELIVERY MAN NOW!
UM... GOOFY, WILL YOU PLEASE STEP OUTSIDE?
TOLD YOU SO, MICK! THEY HID IT OUTSIDE!
I'LL TAKE THAT ICE CREAM NOW!
?
WHAT'S GOING ON?!
YAHOOO!
I'VE BEEN AN IDIOT, MICKEY! BUT WHEN WE ALL REALIZED JUST HOW MUCH GOOFY WANTED A TRAMPOLINE...
GAWRSH! THIS IS MUH BEST BIRTHDAY EVER!
...WE HAD TO ADMIT THAT WHAT GOOFY WANTS IS REALLY AND TRULY WHAT HE NEEDS!
AMEN, SISTER! AND WE ALL NEED GOOFY TO BE GOOFY, TOO!
The End

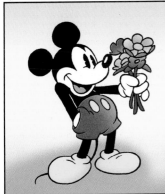

Walt Disney's Mickey Mouse

ENTER... DIPPY DOG!

When Mickey's best friend came to comics in 1933, he was Dippy Dog, public nuisance. He'd respell his last name "Dawg"—and attain closer friendship with Mickey—soon after. But he'd have to wait until 1936 to become Goofy. Gawrsh!

OH, GOSH! HERE COMES THAT PEST, DIPPY DOG!
FWEENG FWONG FWANG-A FWUNG!
ZM 33-01-08
HELLO, DIPPY!
HULLO, MICKEY! HOWDJA LIKE T' HEAR ME PLAY MY MOUTH HARP?
I'D LIKE AWFUL WELL T' PLAY FER YA, I WOULD—BY GOSH—I WOULD! HO! HO! HAW! UH-HUK, UH-HUK! UH-HUK!
GEE, DIPPY, IT'D BE SWELL, ONLY I'VE GOT TO CLEAN THIS WALK!
SHUCKS! I KIN DO THAT IN A JIFFY! HEY YA GOT SOME GASOLINE IN YER GARAGE?
SURE! HELP YOURSELF!
I'M SMART, I AM—BY GOSH—I AM!
? ?
GASOLINE

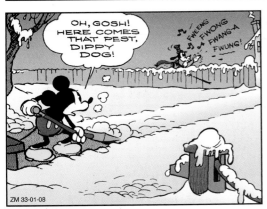

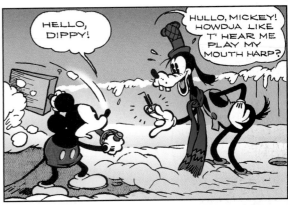

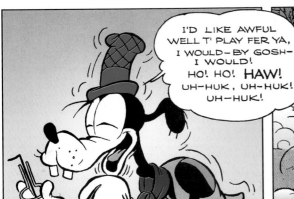

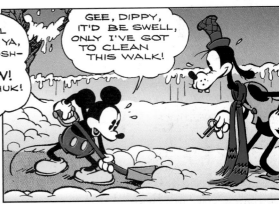

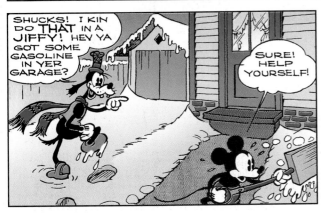

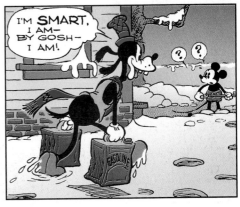

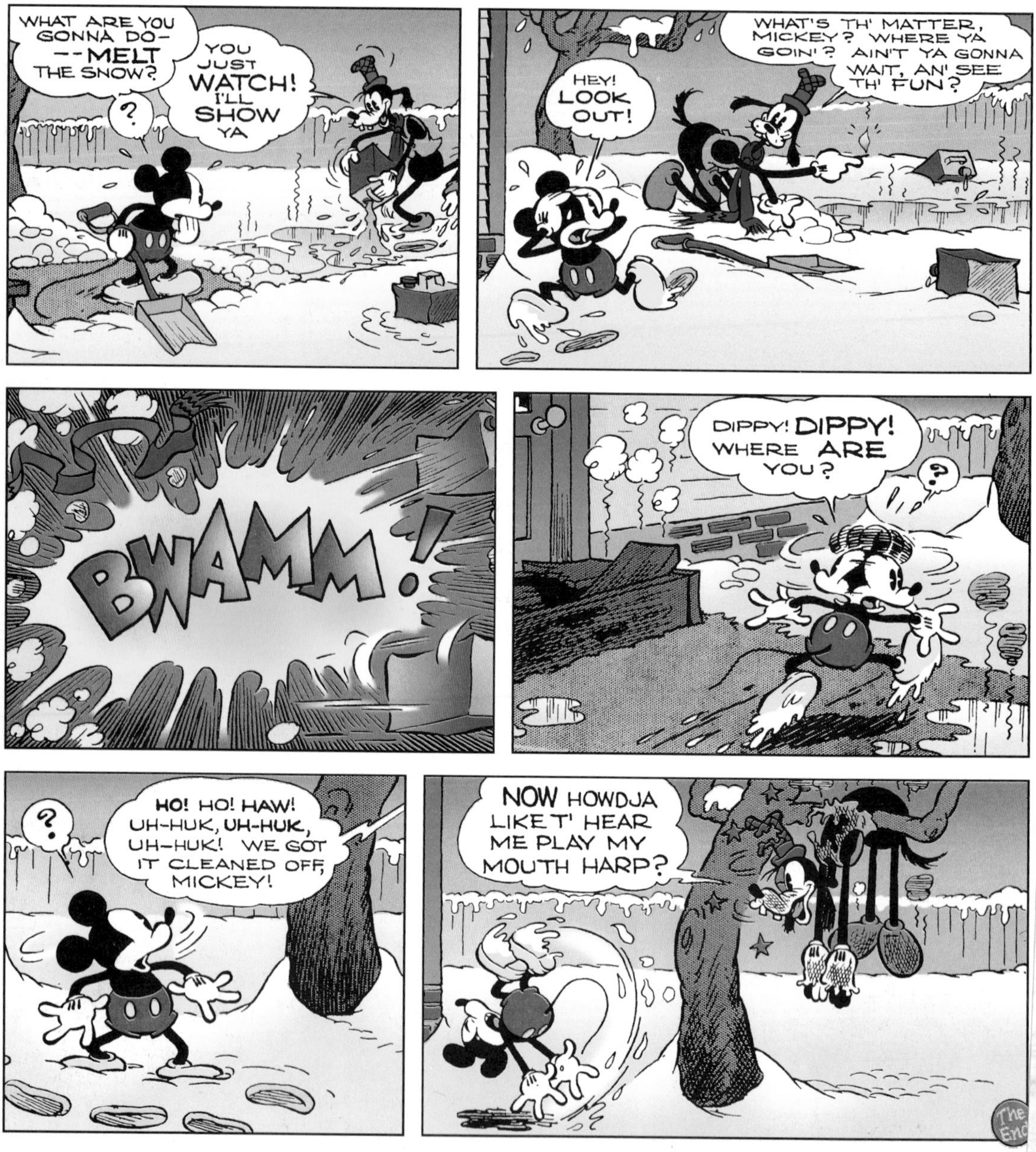
WHAT ARE YOU GONNA DO— --MELT THE SNOW?
?
YOU JUST WATCH! I'LL SHOW YA
WHAT'S TH' MATTER, MICKEY? WHERE YA GOIN'? AIN'T YA GONNA WAIT, AN' SEE TH' FUN?
HEY! LOOK OUT!
BWAMM!
DIPPY! DIPPY! WHERE ARE YOU?
?
?
HO! HO! HAW! UH-HUK, UH-HUK, UH-HUK! WE GOT IT CLEANED OFF, MICKEY!
NOW HOWDJA LIKE T' HEAR ME PLAY MY MOUTH HARP?
The End

SNEAK PREVIEW?

The January 8, 1933 *Mickey Mouse* Sunday strip marked Goofy's debut as a recurring character. But was it his very **first** appearance? Some eight months earlier—in an unrelated Mickey daily strip story—a hungry bumpkin (right) made a one-panel cameo. Though lacking black fur, this hayseed was clearly based on Dippy Dog in his first animated role, *Mickey's Revue* (1932, far right).

—David Gerstein

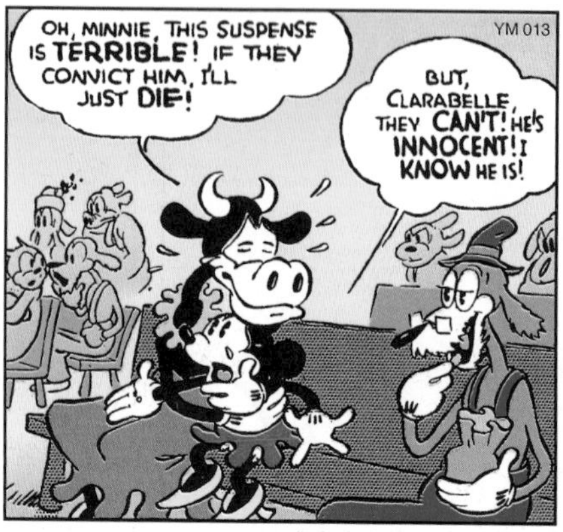
YM 013
OH, MINNIE, THIS SUSPENSE IS TERRIBLE! IF THEY CONVICT HIM, I'LL JUST DIE!
BUT, CLARABELLE, THEY CAN'T! HE'S INNOCENT! I KNOW HE IS!

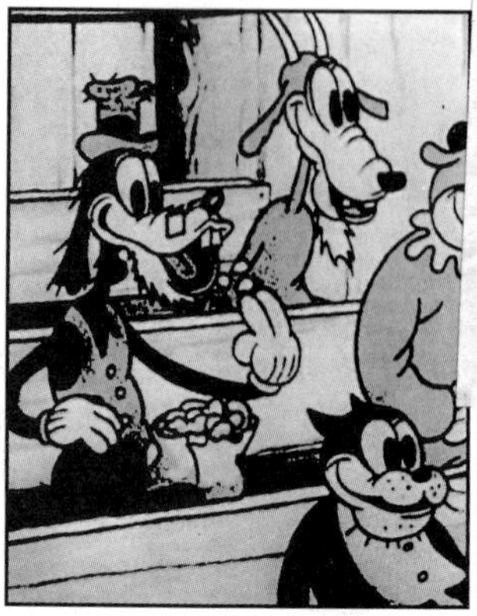

Walt Disney's Donald Duck in Snob's Your Uncle

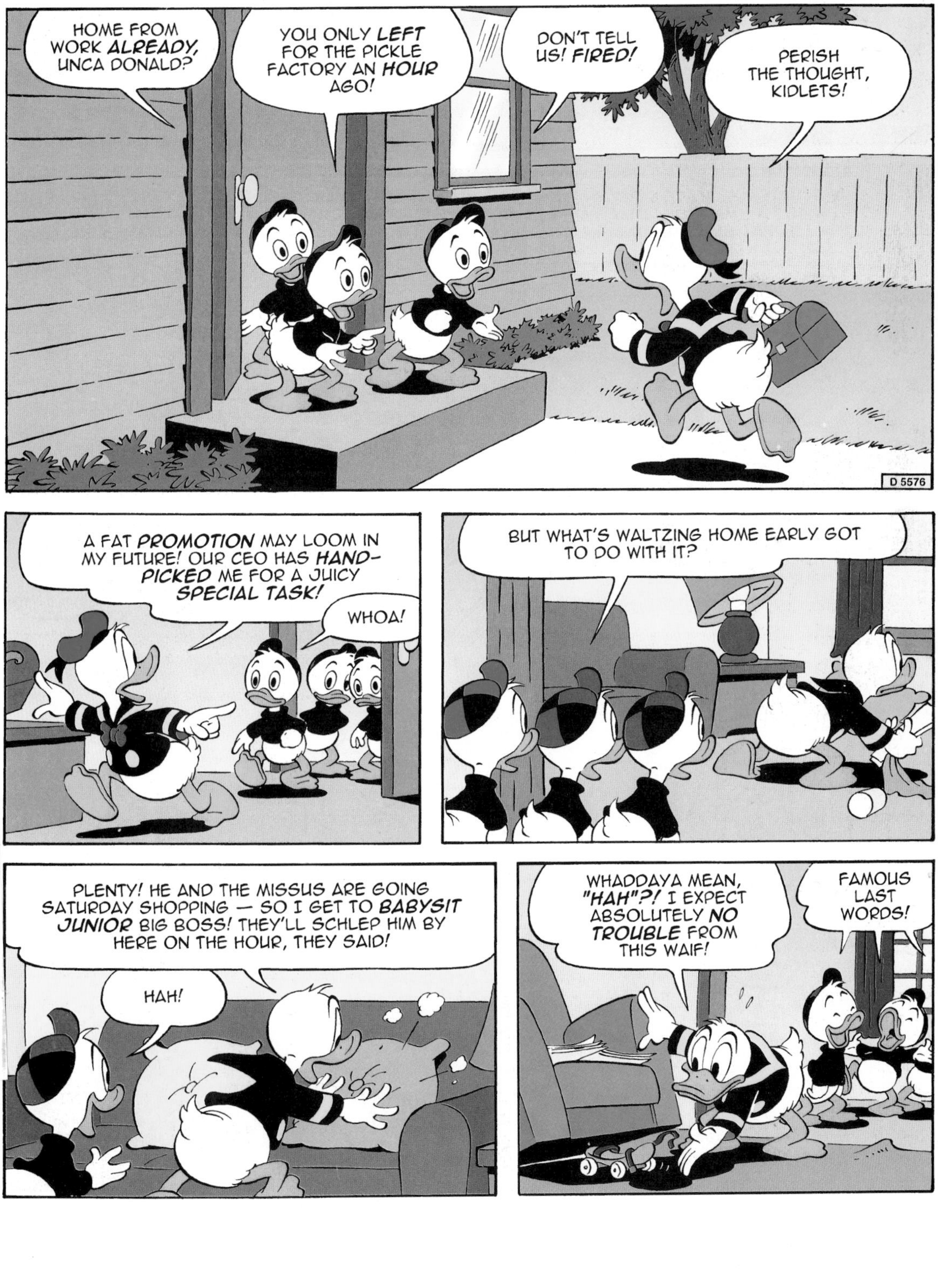
HOME FROM WORK ALREADY, UNCA DONALD?
YOU ONLY LEFT FOR THE PICKLE FACTORY AN HOUR AGO!
DON'T TELL US! FIRED!
PERISH THE THOUGHT, KIDLETS!
D 5576
A FAT PROMOTION MAY LOOM IN MY FUTURE! OUR CEO HAS HAND-PICKED ME FOR A JUICY SPECIAL TASK!
WHOA!
BUT WHAT'S WALTZING HOME EARLY GOT TO DO WITH IT?
PLENTY! HE AND THE MISSUS ARE GOING SATURDAY SHOPPING — SO I GET TO BABYSIT JUNIOR BIG BOSS! THEY'LL SCHLEP HIM BY HERE ON THE HOUR, THEY SAID!
HAH!
WHADDAYA MEAN, "HAH"?! I EXPECT ABSOLUTELY NO TROUBLE FROM THIS WAIF!
FAMOUS LAST WORDS!

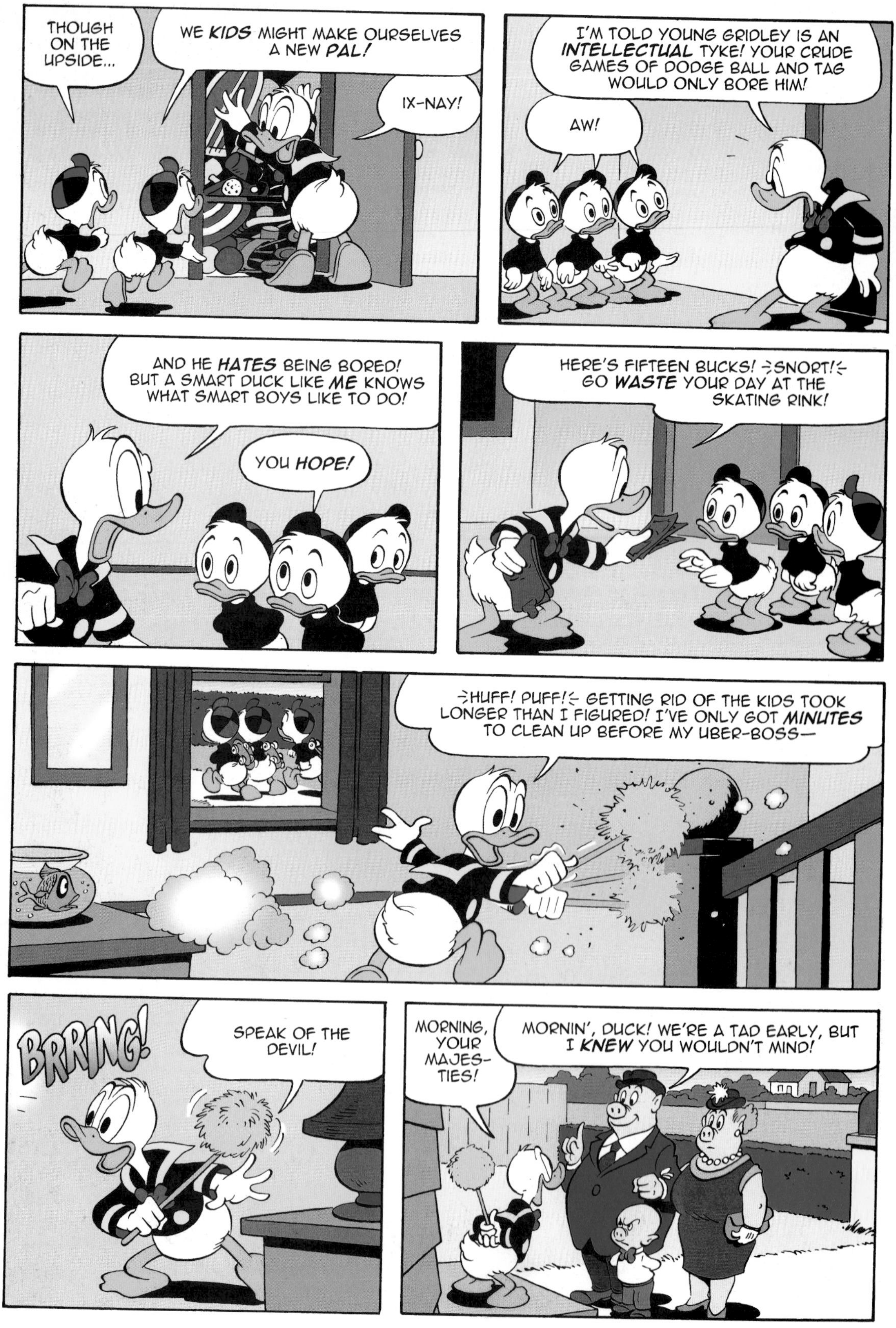
THOUGH ON THE UPSIDE...
WE KIDS MIGHT MAKE OURSELVES A NEW PAL!
IX-NAY!
I'M TOLD YOUNG GRIDLEY IS AN INTELLECTUAL TYKE! YOUR CRUDE GAMES OF DODGE BALL AND TAG WOULD ONLY BORE HIM!
AW!
AND HE HATES BEING BORED! BUT A SMART DUCK LIKE ME KNOWS WHAT SMART BOYS LIKE TO DO!
YOU HOPE!
HERE'S FIFTEEN BUCKS! SNORT! GO WASTE YOUR DAY AT THE SKATING RINK!
HUFF! PUFF! GETTING RID OF THE KIDS TOOK LONGER THAN I FIGURED! I'VE ONLY GOT MINUTES TO CLEAN UP BEFORE MY UBER-BOSS—
BRRING!
SPEAK OF THE DEVIL!
MORNING, YOUR MAJES-TIES!
MORNIN', DUCK! WE'RE A TAD EARLY, BUT I KNEW YOU WOULDN'T MIND!

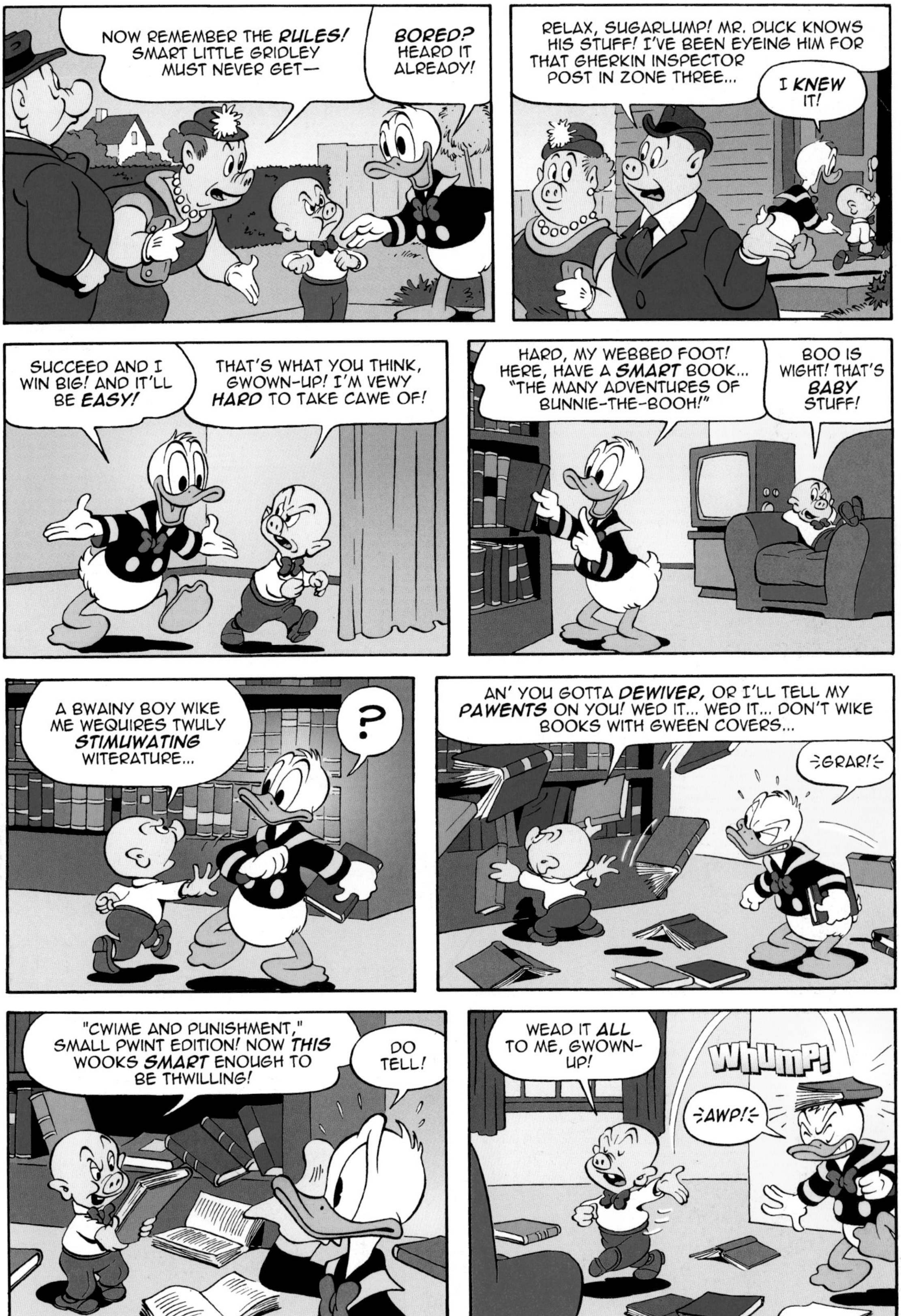
NOW REMEMBER THE RULES! SMART LITTLE GRIDLEY MUST NEVER GET—
BORED? HEARD IT ALREADY!
RELAX, SUGARLUMP! MR. DUCK KNOWS HIS STUFF! I'VE BEEN EYEING HIM FOR THAT GHERKIN INSPECTOR POST IN ZONE THREE...
I KNEW IT!
SUCCEED AND I WIN BIG! AND IT'LL BE EASY!
THAT'S WHAT YOU THINK, GWOWN-UP! I'M VEWY HARD TO TAKE CAWE OF!
HARD, MY WEBBED FOOT! HERE, HAVE A SMART BOOK... "THE MANY ADVENTURES OF BUNNIE-THE-BOOH!"
BOO IS WIGHT! THAT'S BABY STUFF!
A BWAINY BOY WIKE ME WEQUIRES TWULY STIMUWATING WITERATURE...
?
AN' YOU GOTTA DEWIVER, OR I'LL TELL MY PAWENTS ON YOU! WED IT... WED IT... DON'T WIKE BOOKS WITH GWEEN COVERS...
GRAR!
"CWIME AND PUNISHMENT," SMALL PWINT EDITION! NOW THIS WOOKS SMART ENOUGH TO BE THWILLING!
DO TELL!
WEAD IT ALL TO ME, GWOWN-UP!
WHUMP!
AWP!

UMPTEEN CHAPTERS AND TEN JILLION WORDS! BY THE TIME I'M DONE, GLOBAL WARMING WILL FREEZE OVER—
BUT I CAN'T WEAD SMALL PWINT!
IT HURTS MY WITTLE EYES! AN' WHEN I CAN'T WEAD I GET BORED! AN' WHEN I GET BORED I TELL MY PAWENTS...
OPEN UP THOSE PEARLY GATES!
"...WITH SLOW FALTERING STEPS, WITH SHAKING KNEES, RASKOLNIKOV MADE HIS WAY BACK TO HIS LITTLE GARRET..."
AWIGHT! STOP, GWOWN-UP! YOUR WEADING BORES ME! UTTEWLY SPIWITWESS INFWECTION!
WHAT?!
I'D EVEN PWEFER TV... I WOULD, I WOULD!
SNORT!
CLICK!
HUH? HEADWINE NEWS?! I HATE HEADWINE NEWS! ITS UGWY SENSATIONAWISM WACKS WEAL INTEWWECT!
GOOD NIGHT!
AND SIMPLE PWOGWAMS BORE ME! FIND ME A SMARTER SHOW... AN OPEWA!
AW, FOR THE LOVE O'...
BOWLING... WRESTLING... GILBERT AND SULLIVAN! SMART ENOUGH?
I AM THE MONARCH OF THE SEA!

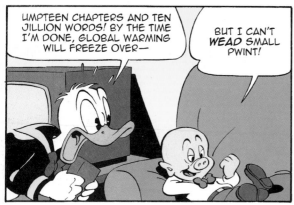

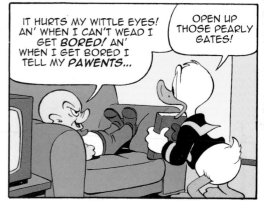

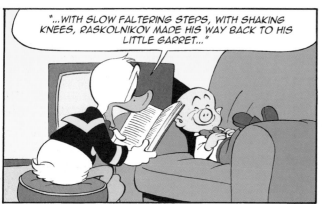

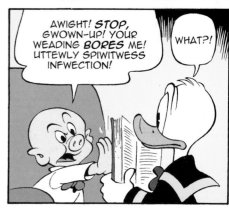

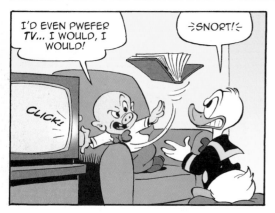

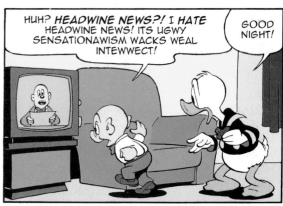

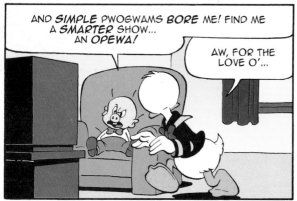

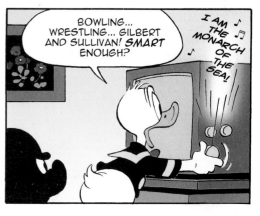

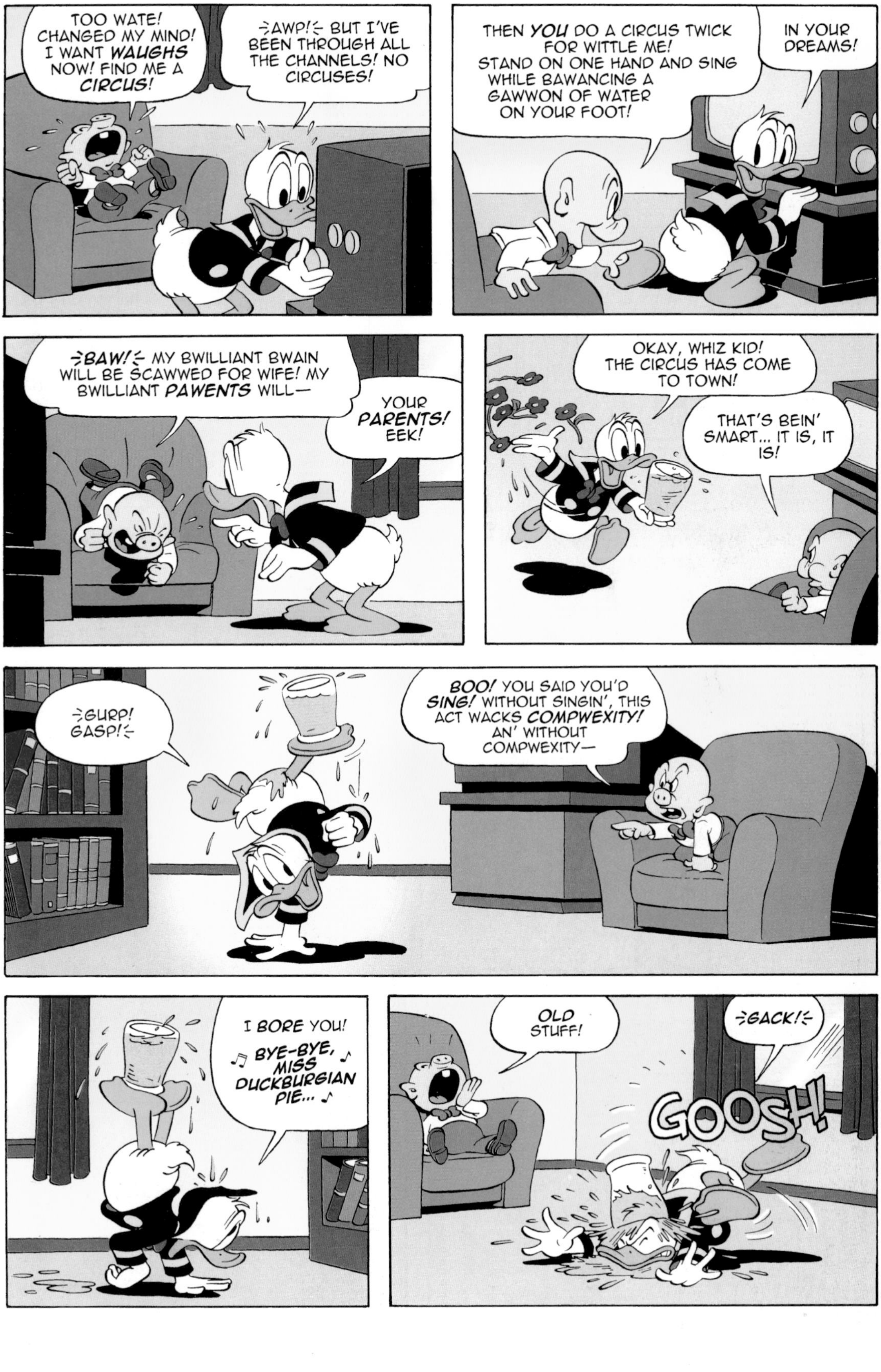
TOO WATE! CHANGED MY MIND! I WANT WAUGHS NOW! FIND ME A CIRCUS!
AWP! BUT I'VE BEEN THROUGH ALL THE CHANNELS! NO CIRCUSES!
THEN YOU DO A CIRCUS TWICK FOR WITTLE ME! STAND ON ONE HAND AND SING WHILE BAWANCING A GAWWON OF WATER ON YOUR FOOT!
IN YOUR DREAMS!
BAW! MY BWILLIANT BWAIN WILL BE SCAWWED FOR WIFE! MY BWILLIANT PAWENTS WILL—
YOUR PARENTS! EEK!
OKAY, WHIZ KID! THE CIRCUS HAS COME TO TOWN!
THAT'S BEIN' SMART... IT IS, IT IS!
GURP! GASP!
BOO! YOU SAID YOU'D SING! WITHOUT SINGIN', THIS ACT WACKS COMPWEXITY! AN' WITHOUT COMPWEXITY—
I BORE YOU!
♫ BYE-BYE, MISS DUCKBURGIAN PIE... ♪
OLD STUFF!
GACK!
GOOSH!

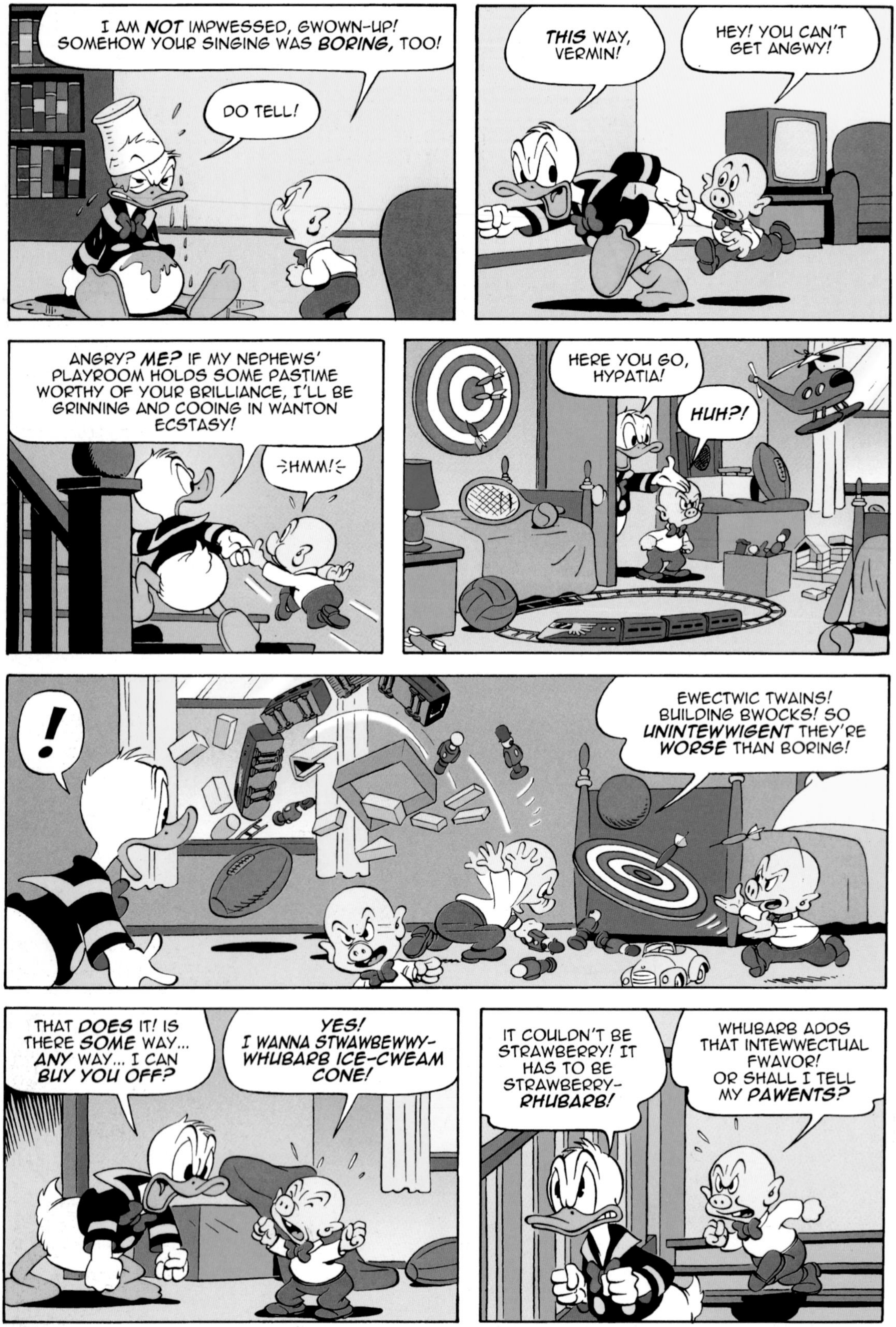
I AM NOT IMPWESSED, GWOWN-UP! SOMEHOW YOUR SINGING WAS BORING, TOO!
DO TELL!
THIS WAY, VERMIN!
HEY! YOU CAN'T GET ANGWY!
ANGRY? ME? IF MY NEPHEWS' PLAYROOM HOLDS SOME PASTIME WORTHY OF YOUR BRILLIANCE, I'LL BE GRINNING AND COOING IN WANTON ECSTASY!
HMM!
HERE YOU GO, HYPATIA!
HUH?!
!
EWECTWIC TWAINS! BUILDING BWOCKS! SO UNINTEWWIGENT THEY'RE WORSE THAN BORING!
THAT DOES IT! IS THERE SOME WAY... ANY WAY... I CAN BUY YOU OFF?
YES! I WANNA STWAWBEWWY-WHUBARB ICE-CWEAM CONE!
IT COULDN'T BE STRAWBERRY! IT HAS TO BE STRAWBERRY-RHUBARB!
WHUBARB ADDS THAT INTEWWECTUAL FWAVOR! OR SHALL I TELL MY PAWENTS?

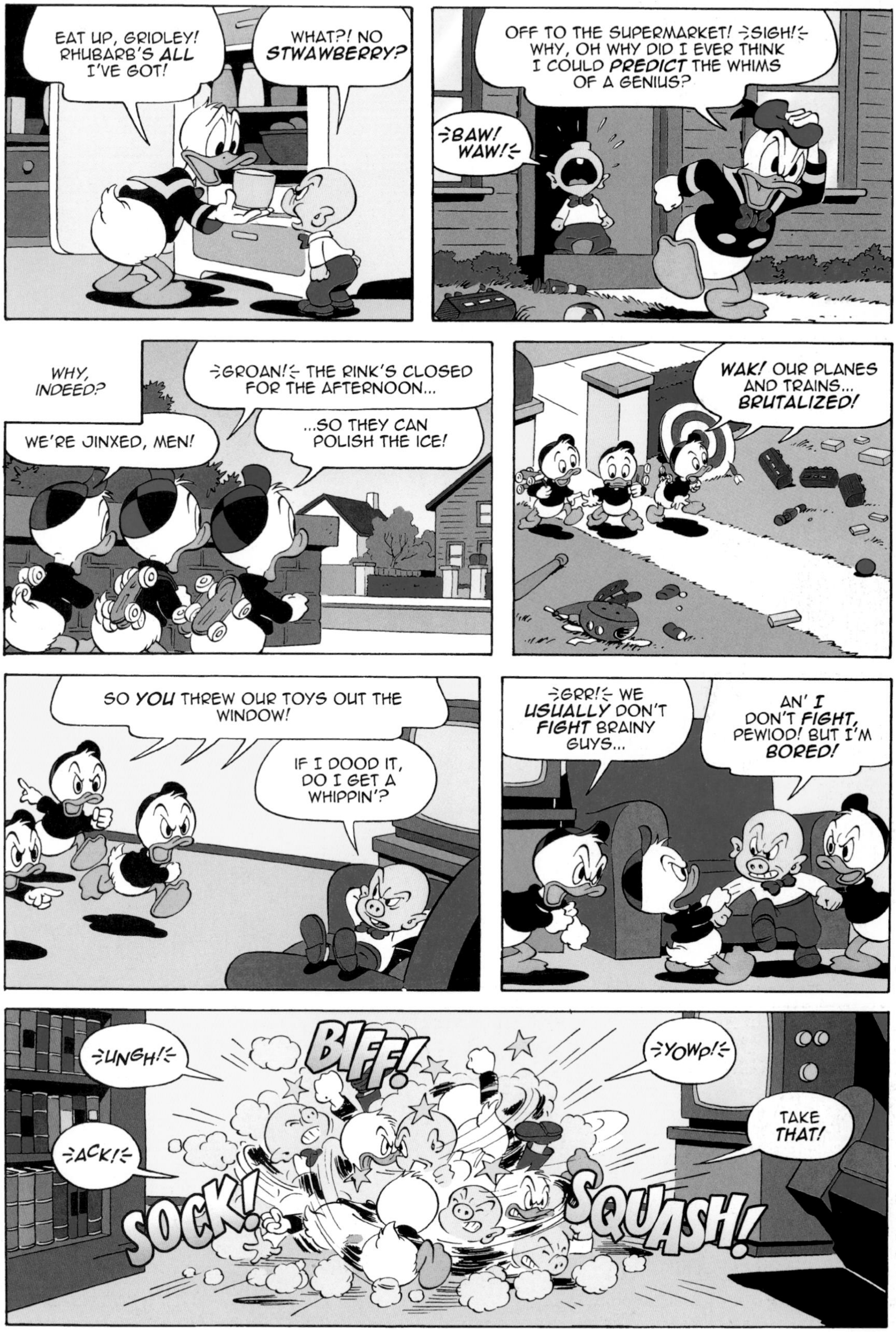
EAT UP, GRIDLEY! RHUBARB'S ALL I'VE GOT!
WHAT?! NO STWAWBERRY?
OFF TO THE SUPERMARKET! SIGH! WHY, OH WHY DID I EVER THINK I COULD PREDICT THE WHIMS OF A GENIUS?
BAW! WAW!
WHY, INDEED?
GROAN! THE RINK'S CLOSED FOR THE AFTERNOON...
WE'RE JINXED, MEN!
...SO THEY CAN POLISH THE ICE!
WAK! OUR PLANES AND TRAINS... BRUTALIZED!
SO YOU THREW OUR TOYS OUT THE WINDOW!
IF I DOOD IT, DO I GET A WHIPPIN'?
GRR! WE USUALLY DON'T FIGHT BRAINY GUYS...
AN' I DON'T FIGHT, PEWIOD! BUT I'M BORED!
UNGH!
BIFF!
YOWP!
ACK!
TAKE THAT!
SOCK!
SQUASH!

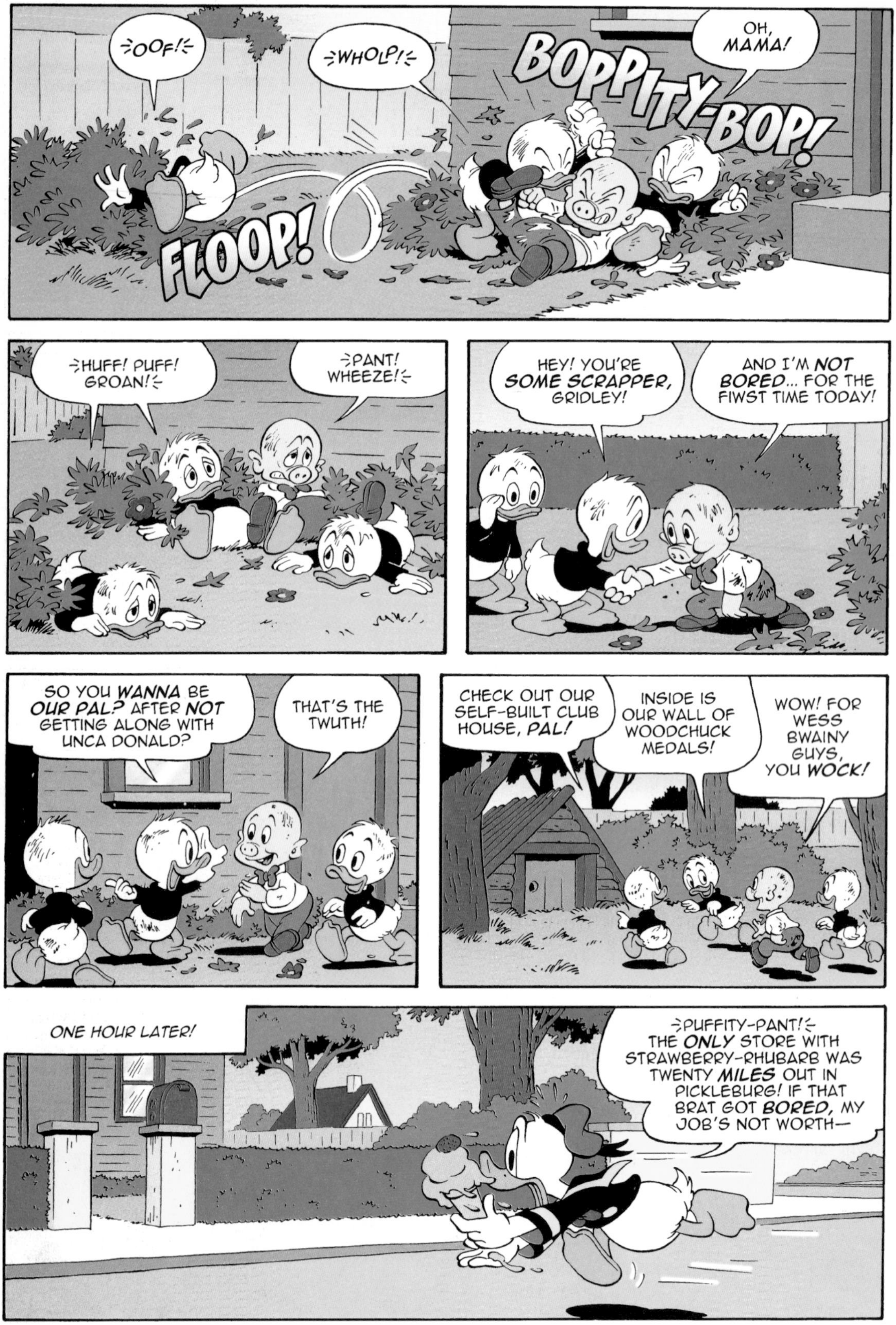

OOF!
WHOLP!
BOPPITY-BOP!
OH, MAMA!
FLOOP!
HUFF! PUFF! GROAN!
PANT! WHEEZE!
HEY! YOU'RE SOME SCRAPPER, GRIDLEY!
AND I'M NOT BORED... FOR THE FIWST TIME TODAY!
SO YOU WANNA BE OUR PAL? AFTER NOT GETTING ALONG WITH UNCA DONALD?
THAT'S THE TWUTH!
CHECK OUT OUR SELF-BUILT CLUB HOUSE, PAL!
INSIDE IS OUR WALL OF WOODCHUCK MEDALS!
WOW! FOR WESS BWAINY GUYS, YOU WOCK!
ONE HOUR LATER!
PUFFITY-PANT! THE ONLY STORE WITH STRAWBERRY-RHUBARB WAS TWENTY MILES OUT IN PICKLEBURG! IF THAT BRAT GOT BORED, MY JOB'S NOT WORTH—

SOCK--- CRASH!

HOLY NED!

MY ETCHED-GLASS WINDOW! ⸱SNORT!⸱ I'M ASHAMED TO BE YOUR UNCLE!

BUT UNCA DONALD! THAT GUY IN YOUR RIGHT FIST ISN'T YOUR NEPHEW—

MR. DUCK! UNHAND OUR GIFTED, DELICATE LITTLE BOY!

⸱EEP!⸱

IT'S AWIGHT, DEAR PAWENTS! I'M NOT AS DEWICATE AS YOU THINK!

!

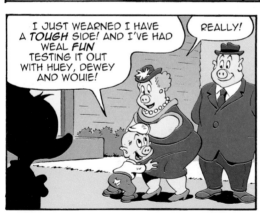

I JUST WEARNED I HAVE A TOUGH SIDE! AND I'VE HAD WEAL FUN TESTING IT OUT WITH HUEY, DEWEY AND WOUIE!

REALLY!

EVEN IF THEIR UNCLE WASN'T EXACTWY ON THE BALL!

⸱PSST!⸱ GOOD ENOUGH FOR ME, DUCK! THAT GHERKIN POSITION IS YOURS!

AND SO...

APES FROM MARS
ALL THIS WEEK

INTELLECT'S JUST WHAT YOU MAKE OF IT, I GUESS! HOW'S THIS MOVIE AS THANKS FOR SAVING MY BACON?

AFTER FORGIVING US FOR FIGHTING AND BREAKING WINDOWS? WE DON'T CARE IF IT'S BORING!

The End

Uncle Scrooge is in another bind. Can Donald and the boys save him from the Peeweegahs? ("What's a Peeweegah," you ask?)

UH OH!

©2007 Disney Enterprises, Inc.

Learn all about Peeweegahs and Wendigos in *Walt Disney's Uncle Scrooge Adventures—The Barks/Rosa Collection.* This new series features stories by famed writers/illustrators Carl Barks and Don Rosa. Each volume contains an original Carl Barks classic followed by a Don Rosa sequel. Volume One kicks things off with "Land of the Pygmy Indians" and "War of the Wendigo." Look for it in July!

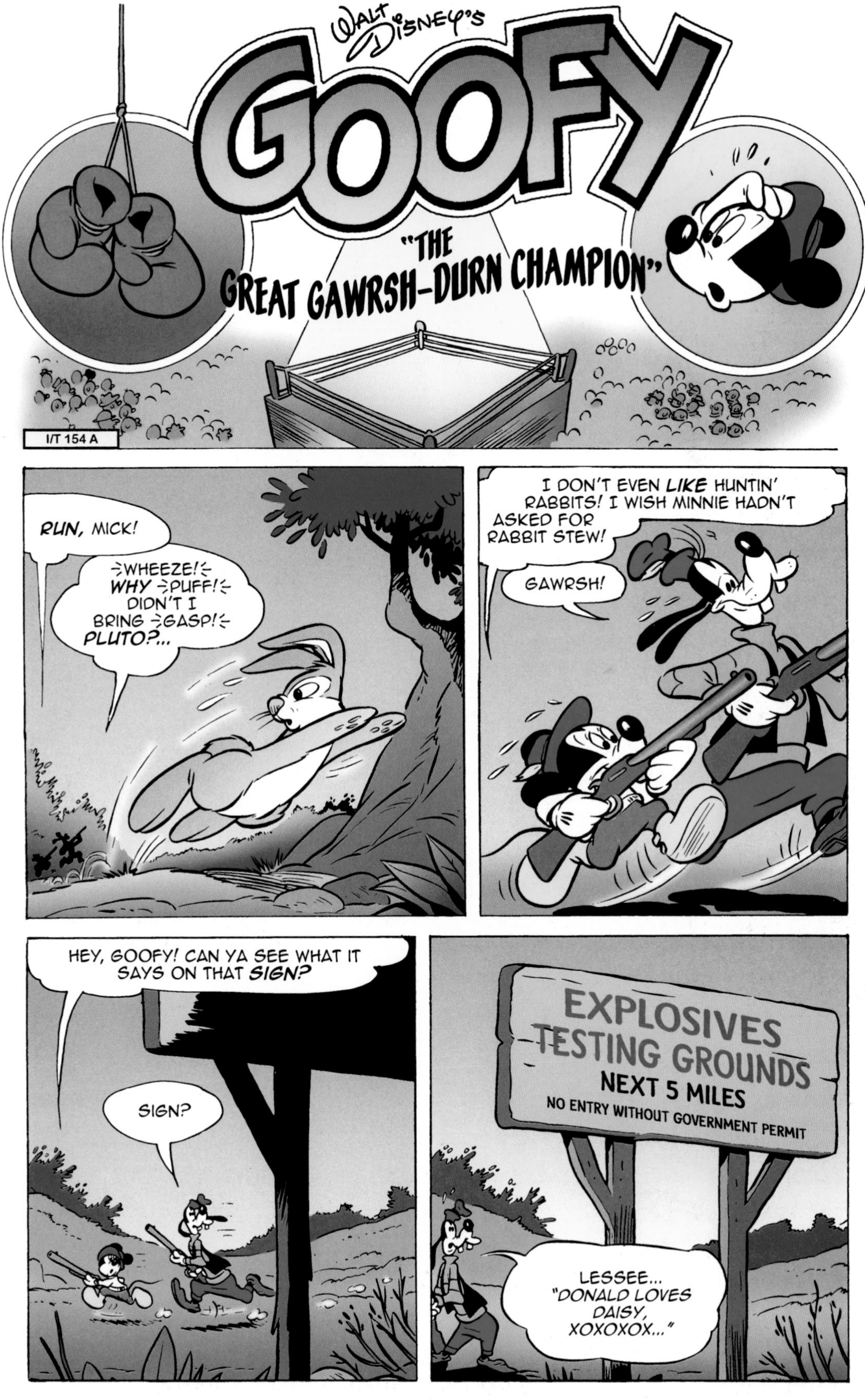
WALT DISNEY'S
GOOFY
"THE GREAT GAWRSH-DURN CHAMPION"
I/T 154 A
RUN, MICK!
WHEEZE! WHY PUFF! DIDN'T I BRING GASP! PLUTO?...
I DON'T EVEN LIKE HUNTIN' RABBITS! I WISH MINNIE HADN'T ASKED FOR RABBIT STEW!
GAWRSH!
HEY, GOOFY! CAN YA SEE WHAT IT SAYS ON THAT SIGN?
SIGN?
EXPLOSIVES TESTING GROUNDS
NEXT 5 MILES
NO ENTRY WITHOUT GOVERNMENT PERMIT
LESSEE... "DONALD LOVES DAISY, XOXOXOX..."

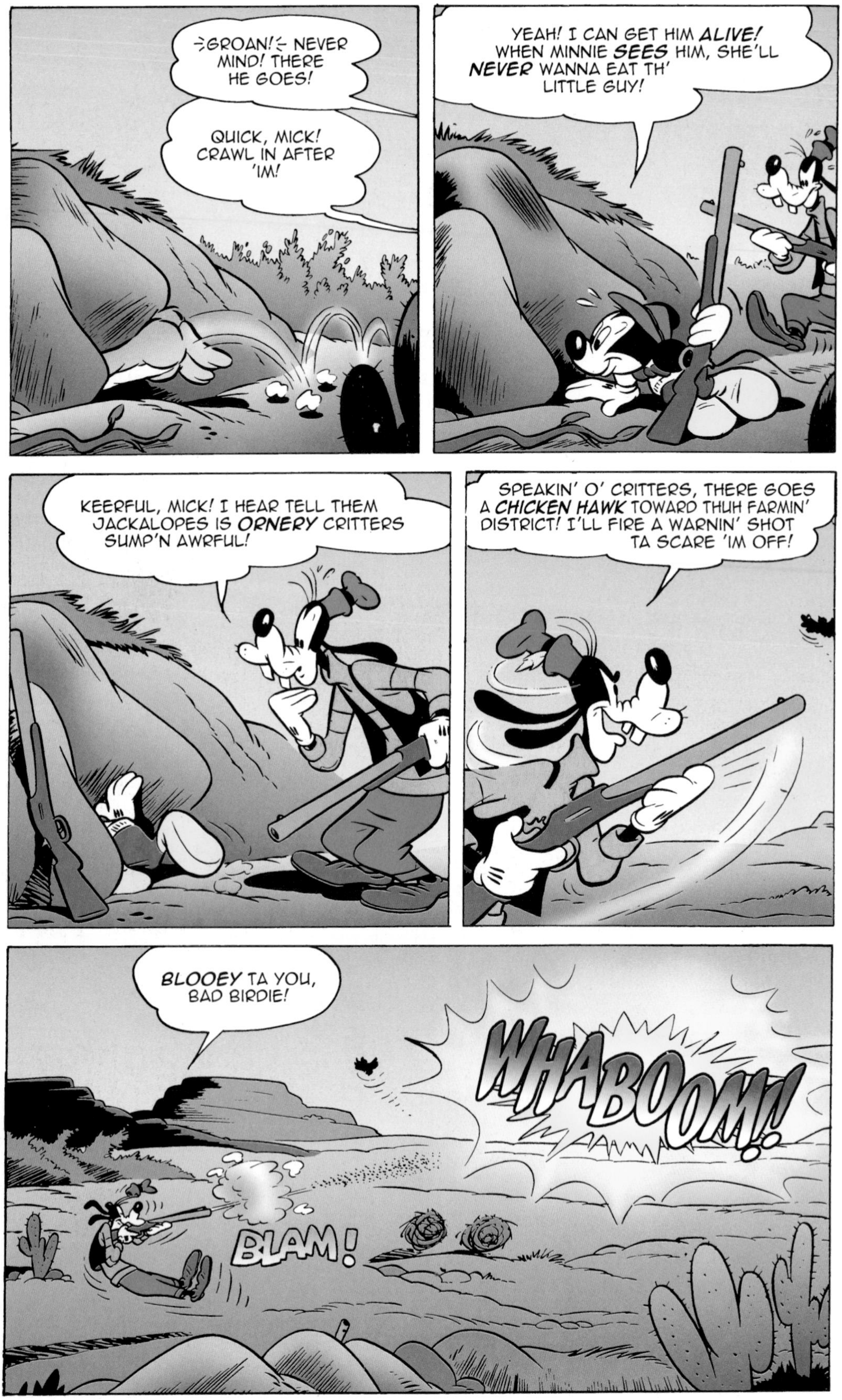
GROAN! NEVER MIND! THERE HE GOES!
QUICK, MICK! CRAWL IN AFTER 'IM!
YEAH! I CAN GET HIM ALIVE! WHEN MINNIE SEES HIM, SHE'LL NEVER WANNA EAT TH' LITTLE GUY!
KEERFUL, MICK! I HEAR TELL THEM JACKALOPES IS ORNERY CRITTERS SUMP'N AWRFUL!
SPEAKIN' O' CRITTERS, THERE GOES A CHICKEN HAWK TOWARD THUH FARMIN' DISTRICT! I'LL FIRE A WARNIN' SHOT TA SCARE 'IM OFF!
BLOOEY TA YOU, BAD BIRDIE!
WHABOOM!!
BLAM!

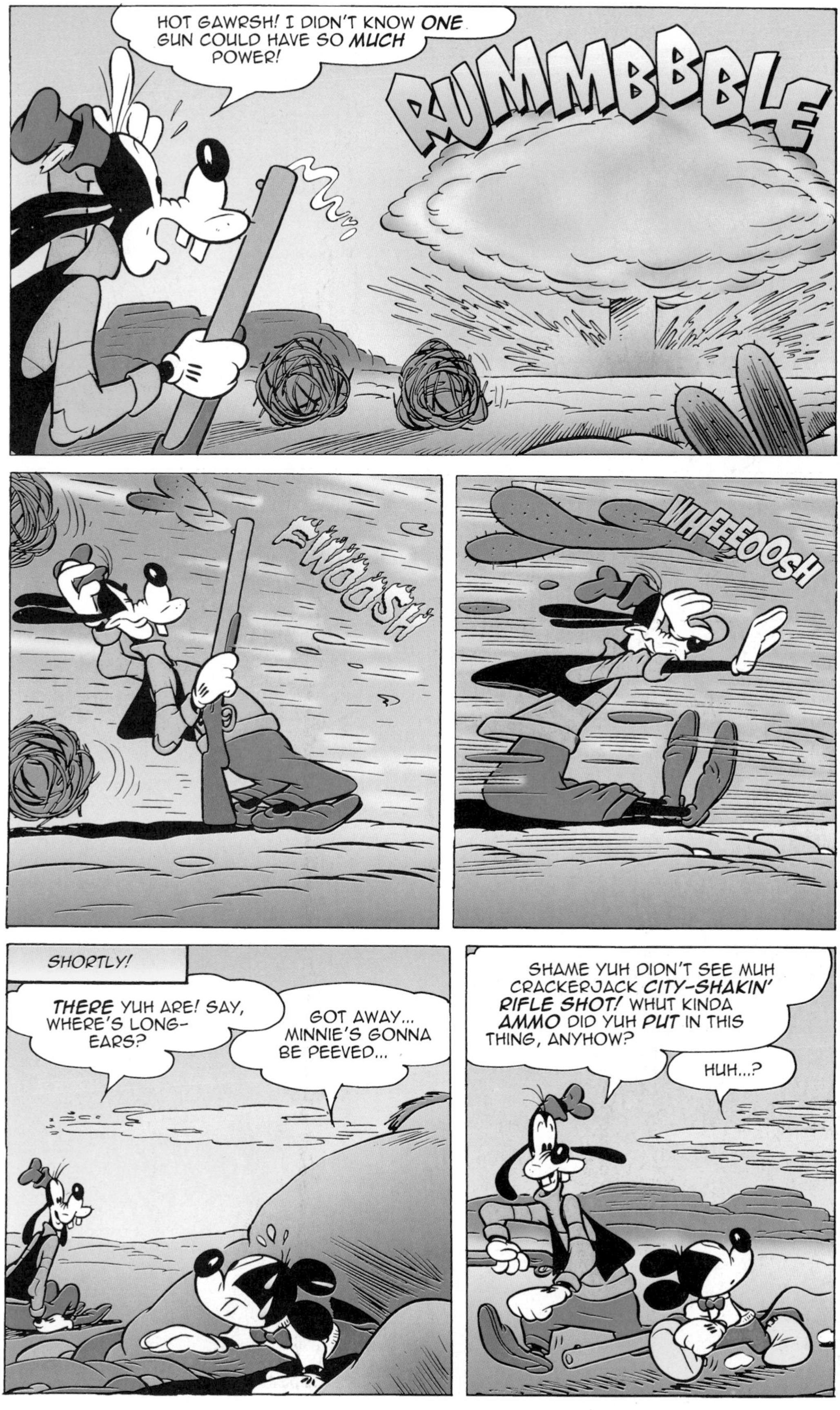

HOT GAWRSH! I DIDN'T KNOW ONE GUN COULD HAVE SO MUCH POWER!
RUMMBBBLE
FWOOSH
WHEEEOOSH
SHORTLY!
THERE YUH ARE! SAY, WHERE'S LONG-EARS?
GOT AWAY... MINNIE'S GONNA BE PEEVED...
SHAME YUH DIDN'T SEE MUH CRACKERJACK CITY-SHAKIN' RIFLE SHOT! WHUT KINDA AMMO DID YUH PUT IN THIS THING, ANYHOW?
HUH...?

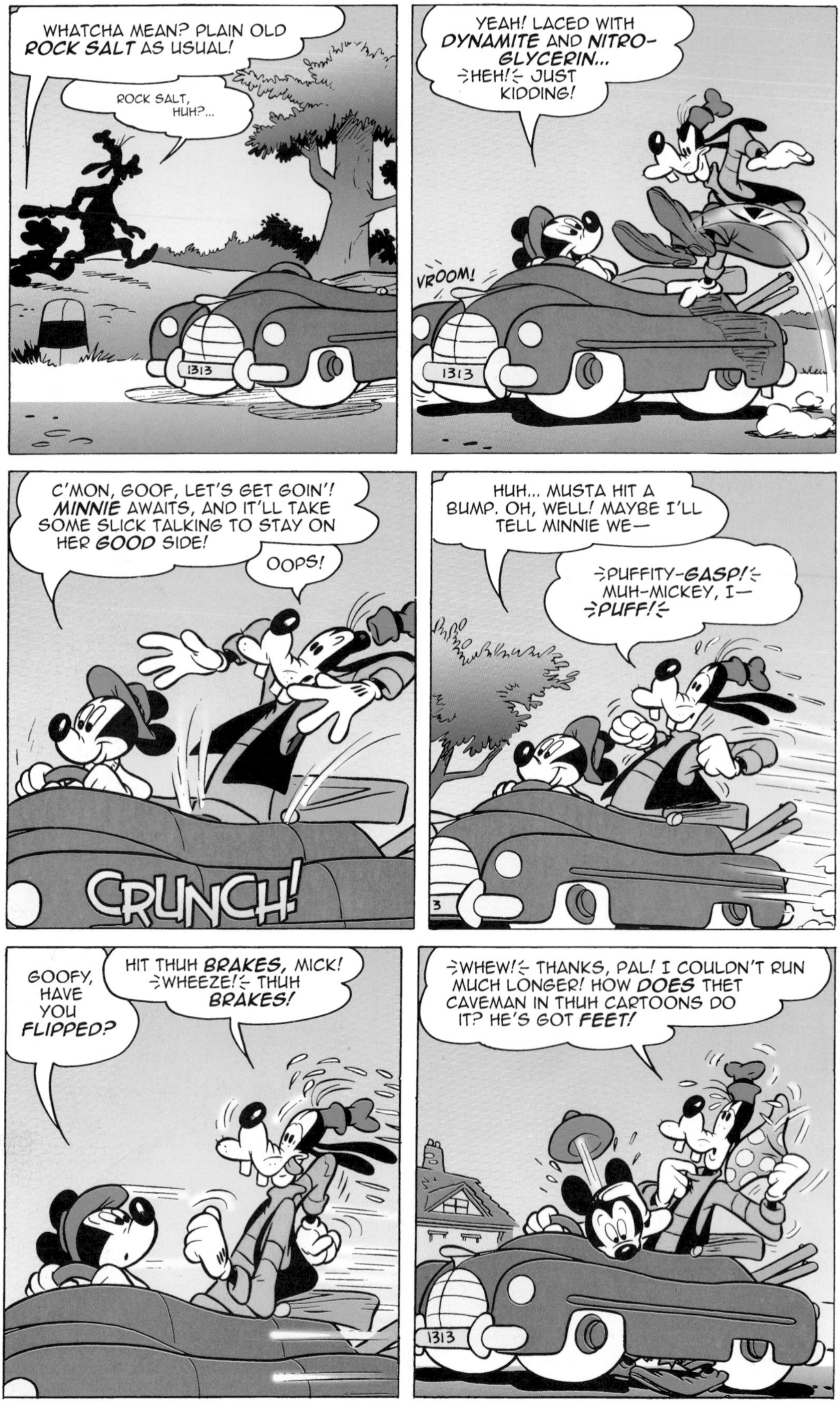
WHATCHA MEAN? PLAIN OLD ROCK SALT AS USUAL!
ROCK SALT, HUH?...
YEAH! LACED WITH DYNAMITE AND NITRO-GLYCERIN... HEH! JUST KIDDING!
VROOM!
1313
C'MON, GOOF, LET'S GET GOIN'! MINNIE AWAITS, AND IT'LL TAKE SOME SLICK TALKING TO STAY ON HER GOOD SIDE!
OOPS!
CRUNCH!
HUH... MUSTA HIT A BUMP. OH, WELL! MAYBE I'LL TELL MINNIE WE—
PUFFITY-GASP! MUH-MICKEY, I— PUFF!
GOOFY, HAVE YOU FLIPPED?
HIT THUH BRAKES, MICK! WHEEZE! THUH BRAKES!
WHEW! THANKS, PAL! I COULDN'T RUN MUCH LONGER! HOW DOES THET CAVEMAN IN THUH CARTOONS DO IT? HE'S GOT FEET!
1313

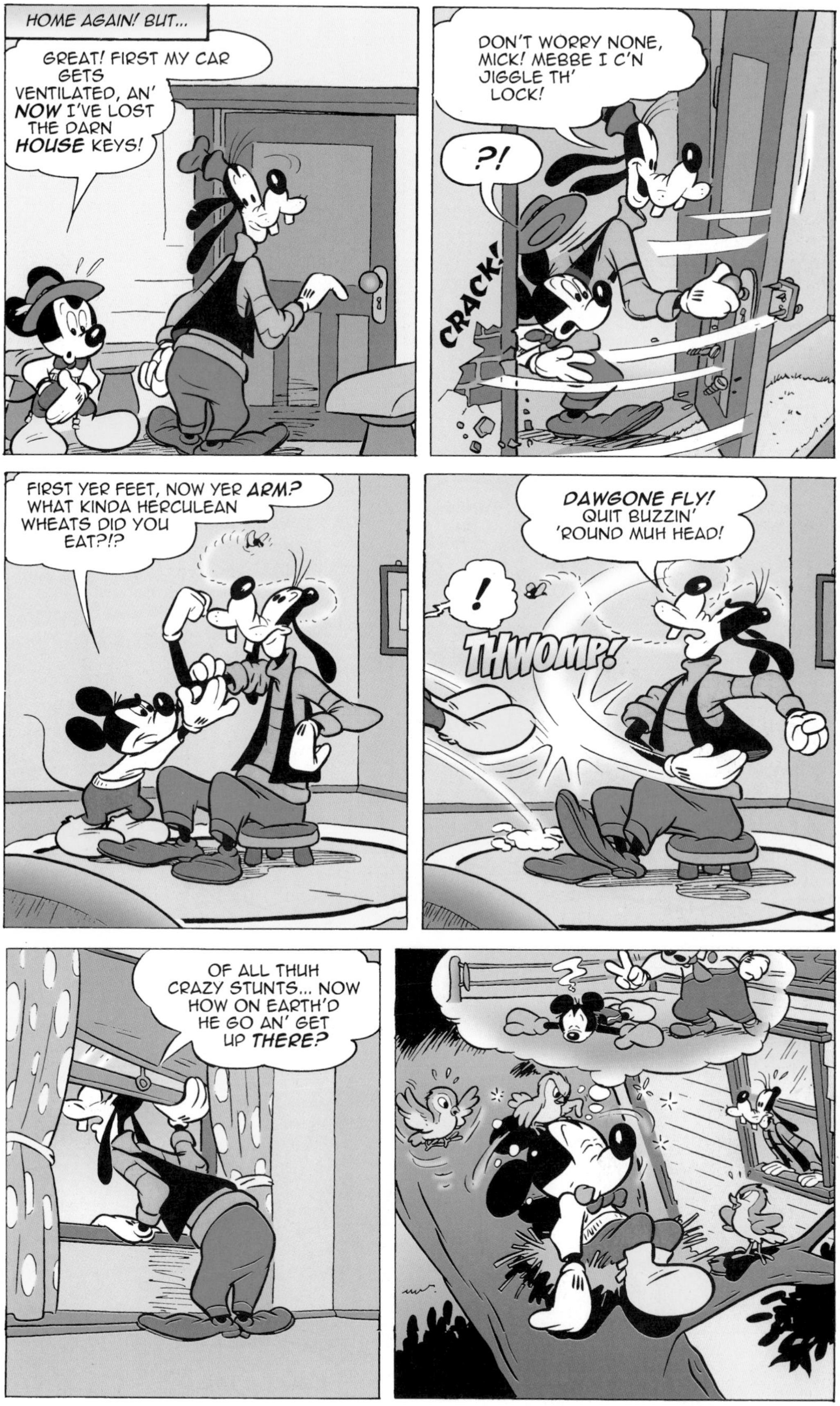
HOME AGAIN! BUT...
GREAT! FIRST MY CAR GETS VENTILATED, AN' NOW I'VE LOST THE DARN HOUSE KEYS!
DON'T WORRY NONE, MICK! MEBBE I C'N JIGGLE TH' LOCK!
?!
CRACK!
FIRST YER FEET, NOW YER ARM? WHAT KINDA HERCULEAN WHEATS DID YOU EAT?!?
DAWGONE FLY! QUIT BUZZIN' 'ROUND MUH HEAD!
!
THWOMP!
OF ALL THUH CRAZY STUNTS... NOW HOW ON EARTH'D HE GO AN' GET UP THERE?

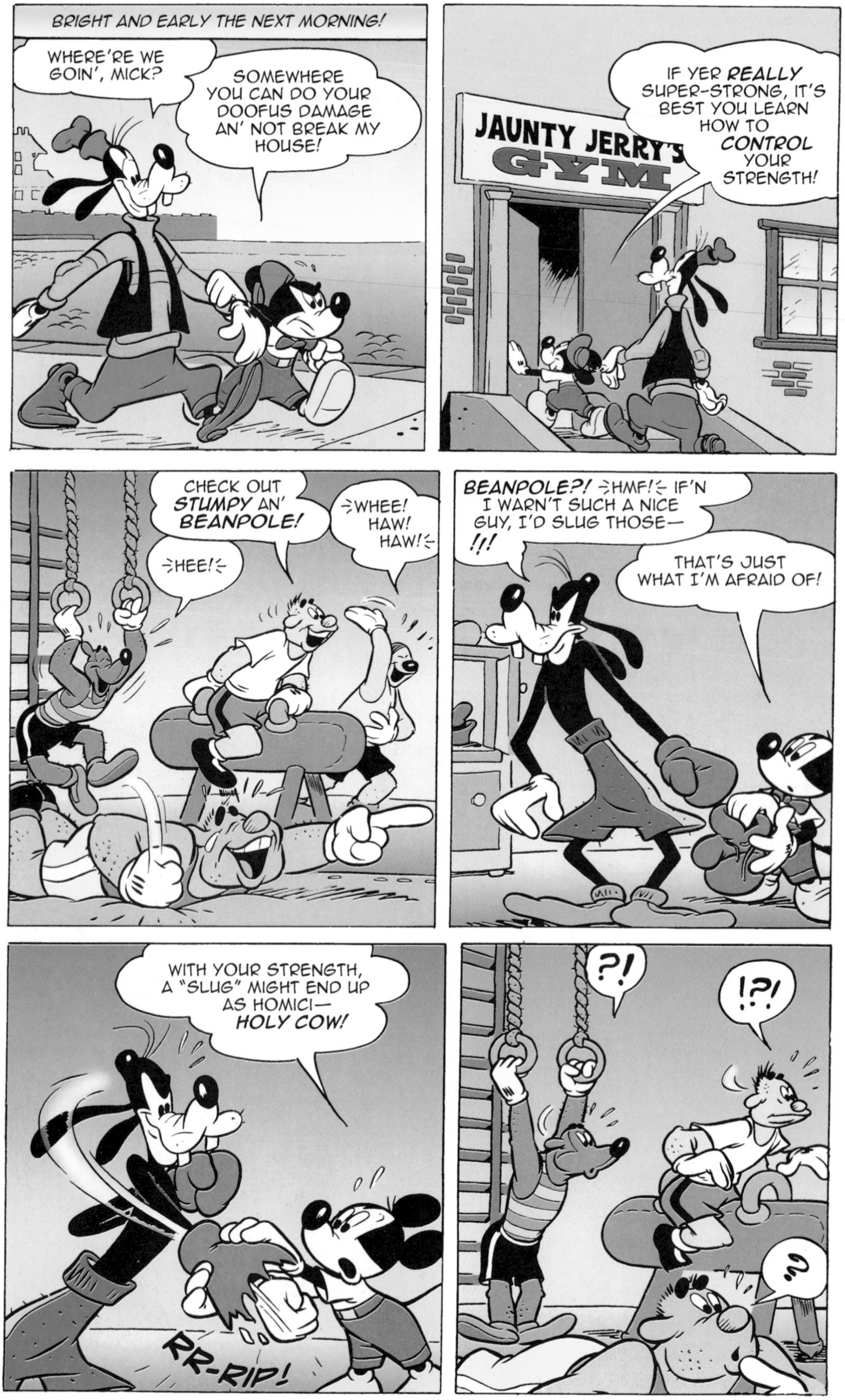
BRIGHT AND EARLY THE NEXT MORNING!
WHERE'RE WE GOIN', MICK?
SOMEWHERE YOU CAN DO YOUR DOOFUS DAMAGE AN' NOT BREAK MY HOUSE!
JAUNTY JERRY'S GYM
IF YER REALLY SUPER-STRONG, IT'S BEST YOU LEARN HOW TO CONTROL YOUR STRENGTH!
CHECK OUT STUMPY AN' BEANPOLE!
WHEE! HAW! HAW!
HEE!
BEANPOLE?! HMF! IF'N I WARN'T SUCH A NICE GUY, I'D SLUG THOSE— !!!
THAT'S JUST WHAT I'M AFRAID OF!
WITH YOUR STRENGTH, A "SLUG" MIGHT END UP AS HOMICI— HOLY COW!
RR-RIP!
?!
!?!
?

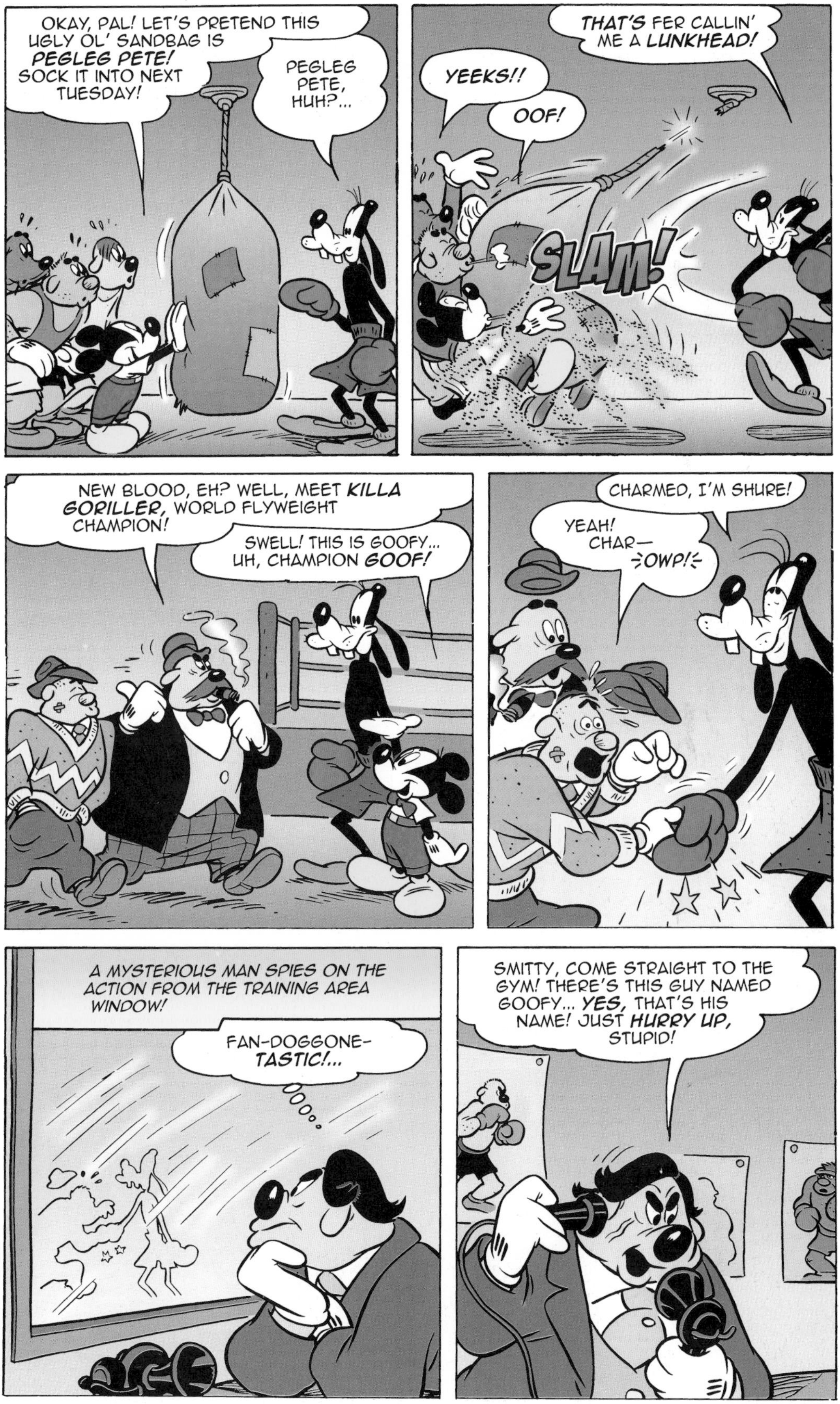
OKAY, PAL! LET'S PRETEND THIS UGLY OL' SANDBAG IS ***PEGLEG PETE!*** SOCK IT INTO NEXT TUESDAY!
PEGLEG PETE, HUH?...
THAT'S FER CALLIN' ME A ***LUNKHEAD!***
YEEKS!!
OOF!
SLAM!
NEW BLOOD, EH? WELL, MEET ***KILLA GORILLER,*** WORLD FLYWEIGHT CHAMPION!
SWELL! THIS IS GOOFY... UH, CHAMPION ***GOOF!***
CHARMED, I'M SHURE!
YEAH! CHAR— ***OWP!***
A MYSTERIOUS MAN SPIES ON THE ACTION FROM THE TRAINING AREA WINDOW!
FAN-DOGGONE-***TASTIC!...***
SMITTY, COME STRAIGHT TO THE GYM! THERE'S THIS GUY NAMED GOOFY... ***YES,*** THAT'S HIS NAME! JUST ***HURRY UP,*** STUPID!

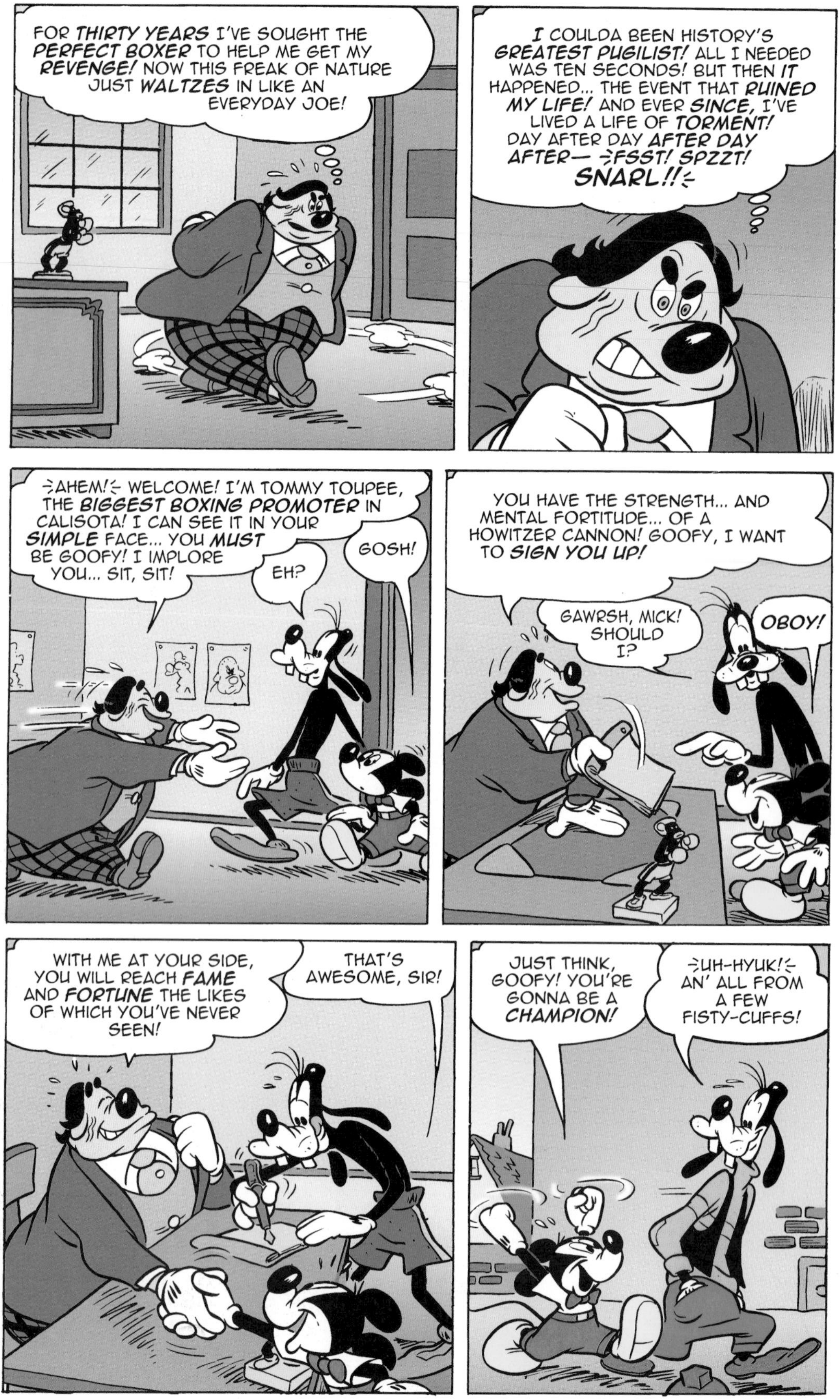
FOR THIRTY YEARS I'VE SOUGHT THE PERFECT BOXER TO HELP ME GET MY REVENGE! NOW THIS FREAK OF NATURE JUST WALTZES IN LIKE AN EVERYDAY JOE!
I COULDA BEEN HISTORY'S GREATEST PUGILIST! ALL I NEEDED WAS TEN SECONDS! BUT THEN IT HAPPENED... THE EVENT THAT RUINED MY LIFE! AND EVER SINCE, I'VE LIVED A LIFE OF TORMENT! DAY AFTER DAY AFTER DAY AFTER— ⥱FSST! SPZZT! SNARL!!⥲
⥱AHEM!⥲ WELCOME! I'M TOMMY TOUPEE, THE BIGGEST BOXING PROMOTER IN CALISOTA! I CAN SEE IT IN YOUR SIMPLE FACE... YOU MUST BE GOOFY! I IMPLORE YOU... SIT, SIT!
EH?
GOSH!
YOU HAVE THE STRENGTH... AND MENTAL FORTITUDE... OF A HOWITZER CANNON! GOOFY, I WANT TO SIGN YOU UP!
GAWRSH, MICK! SHOULD I?
OBOY!
WITH ME AT YOUR SIDE, YOU WILL REACH FAME AND FORTUNE THE LIKES OF WHICH YOU'VE NEVER SEEN!
THAT'S AWESOME, SIR!
JUST THINK, GOOFY! YOU'RE GONNA BE A CHAMPION!
⥱UH-HYUK!⥲ AN' ALL FROM A FEW FISTY-CUFFS!

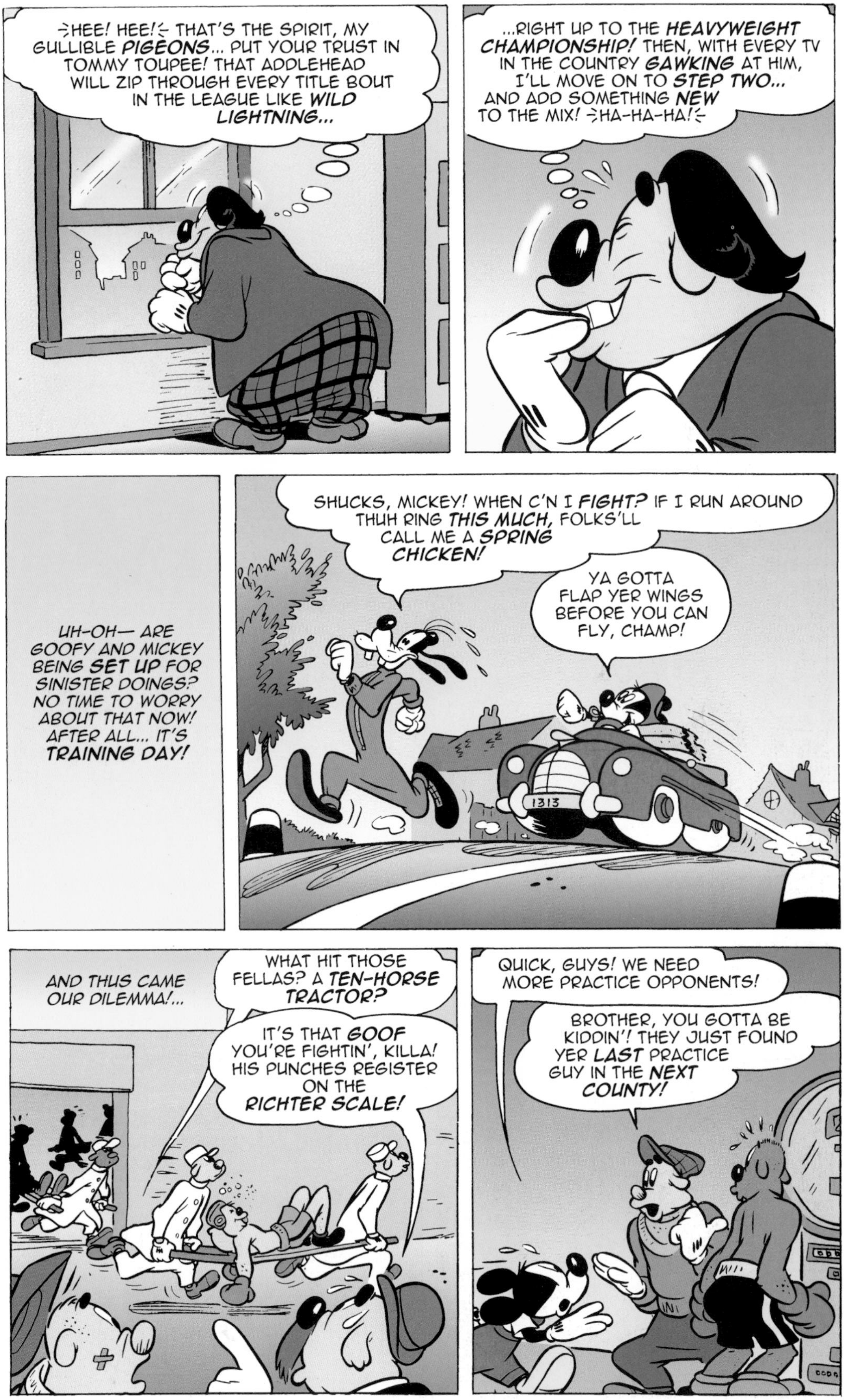

HEE! HEE! THAT'S THE SPIRIT, MY GULLIBLE PIGEONS... PUT YOUR TRUST IN TOMMY TOUPEE! THAT ADDLEHEAD WILL ZIP THROUGH EVERY TITLE BOUT IN THE LEAGUE LIKE WILD LIGHTNING...
...RIGHT UP TO THE HEAVYWEIGHT CHAMPIONSHIP! THEN, WITH EVERY TV IN THE COUNTRY GAWKING AT HIM, I'LL MOVE ON TO STEP TWO... AND ADD SOMETHING NEW TO THE MIX! HA-HA-HA!
UH-OH— ARE GOOFY AND MICKEY BEING SET UP FOR SINISTER DOINGS? NO TIME TO WORRY ABOUT THAT NOW! AFTER ALL... IT'S TRAINING DAY!
SHUCKS, MICKEY! WHEN C'N I FIGHT? IF I RUN AROUND THUH RING THIS MUCH, FOLKS'LL CALL ME A SPRING CHICKEN!
YA GOTTA FLAP YER WINGS BEFORE YOU CAN FLY, CHAMP!
1313
AND THUS CAME OUR DILEMMA!...
WHAT HIT THOSE FELLAS? A TEN-HORSE TRACTOR?
IT'S THAT GOOF YOU'RE FIGHTIN', KILLA! HIS PUNCHES REGISTER ON THE RICHTER SCALE!
QUICK, GUYS! WE NEED MORE PRACTICE OPPONENTS!
BROTHER, YOU GOTTA BE KIDDIN'! THEY JUST FOUND YER LAST PRACTICE GUY IN THE NEXT COUNTY!

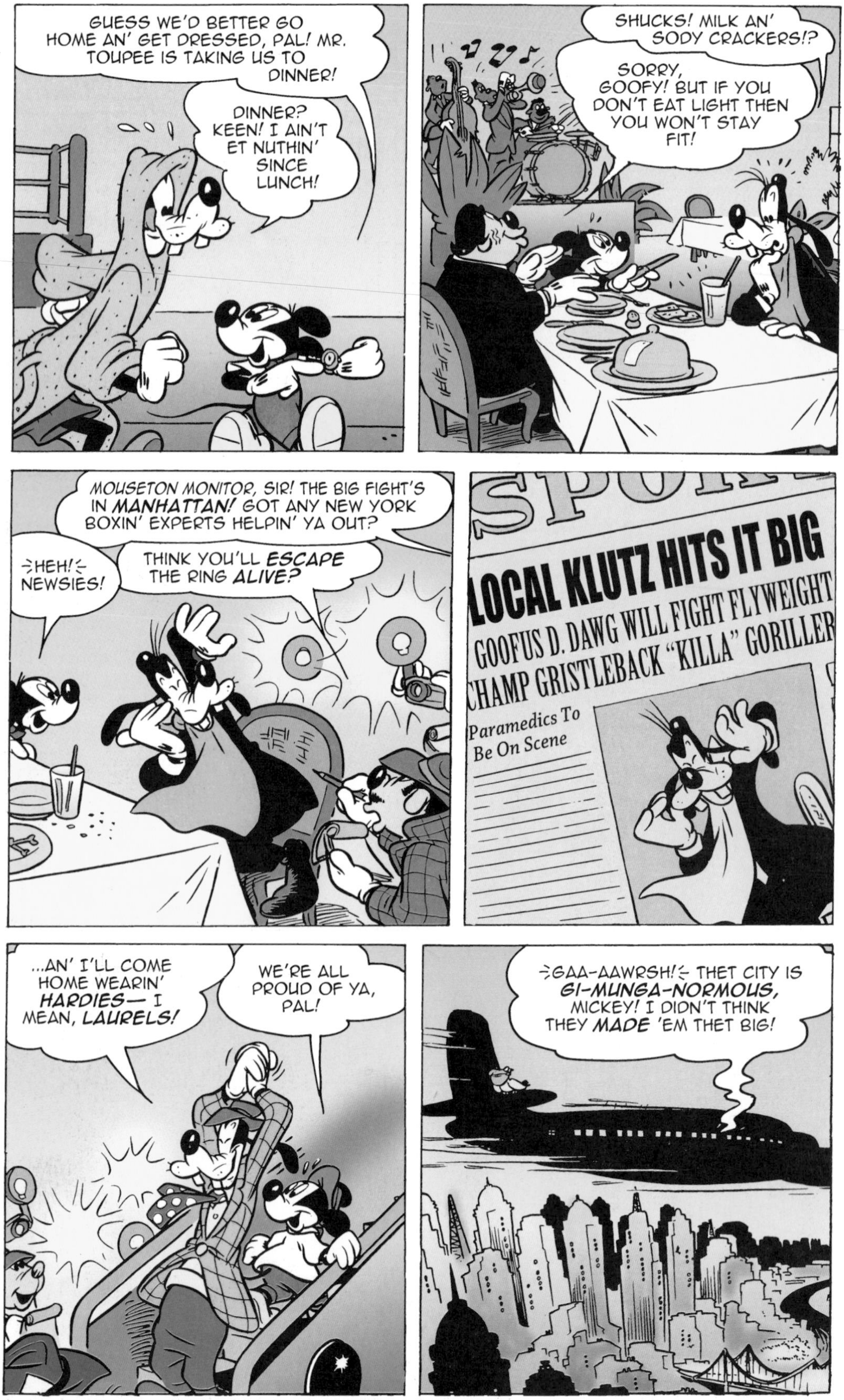
GUESS WE'D BETTER GO HOME AN' GET DRESSED, PAL! MR. TOUPEE IS TAKING US TO DINNER!
DINNER? KEEN! I AIN'T ET NUTHIN' SINCE LUNCH!
SHUCKS! MILK AN' SODY CRACKERS!?
SORRY, GOOFY! BUT IF YOU DON'T EAT LIGHT THEN YOU WON'T STAY FIT!
MOUSETON MONITOR, SIR! THE BIG FIGHT'S IN MANHATTAN! GOT ANY NEW YORK BOXIN' EXPERTS HELPIN' YA OUT?
HEH! NEWSIES!
THINK YOU'LL ESCAPE THE RING ALIVE?
SPORTS
LOCAL KLUTZ HITS IT BIG
GOOFUS D. DAWG WILL FIGHT FLYWEIGHT CHAMP GRISTLEBACK "KILLA" GORILLER
Paramedics To Be On Scene
...AN' I'LL COME HOME WEARIN' HARDIES— I MEAN, LAURELS!
WE'RE ALL PROUD OF YA, PAL!
GAA-AAWRSH! THET CITY IS GI-MUNGA-NORMOUS, MICKEY! I DIDN'T THINK THEY MADE 'EM THET BIG!

NOW SEE THAT WIDE BUILDING AMONG THE SKYSCRAPERS, GOOFY! THAT'S *DAMISON SQUARE GREENHOUSE!* THE GREATEST *SOMEBODIES* IN THE WORLD GO THERE TO BOX!

I COULD BE A GREAT GAWRSH-DURN *CHAMPION!*

A *CHAMPION!* A *SOMEBODY!* IT'S ALL HUMBLE GOOFY COULD WANT! BUT LIFE ISN'T ENTIRELY MILK AND HONEY...

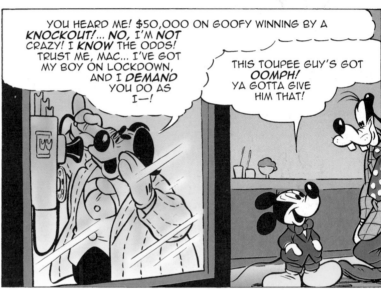

YOU HEARD ME! $50,000 ON GOOFY WINNING BY A *KNOCKOUT!*... *NO,* I'M *NOT* CRAZY! I *KNOW* THE ODDS! TRUST ME, MAC... I'VE GOT MY BOY ON LOCKDOWN, AND I *DEMAND* YOU DO AS I—!

THIS TOUPEE GUY'S GOT *OOMPH!* YA GOTTA GIVE HIM THAT!

WHADDAYA SAY, MICKEY? WANNA PUT DOWN A FEW CLAMS ON GOOFY TO WIN? IT'S A SURE BET...

UH, NO THANKS, MR. TOUPEE! I DON'T BET! BUT MAYBE GOOFY—

SHURE! HOW 'BOUT I PUT DOWN THUH *NICKEL* I BEEN SAVIN' IN MUH POCKET ALL WEEK? I'M GONNER GIT *RICH!*

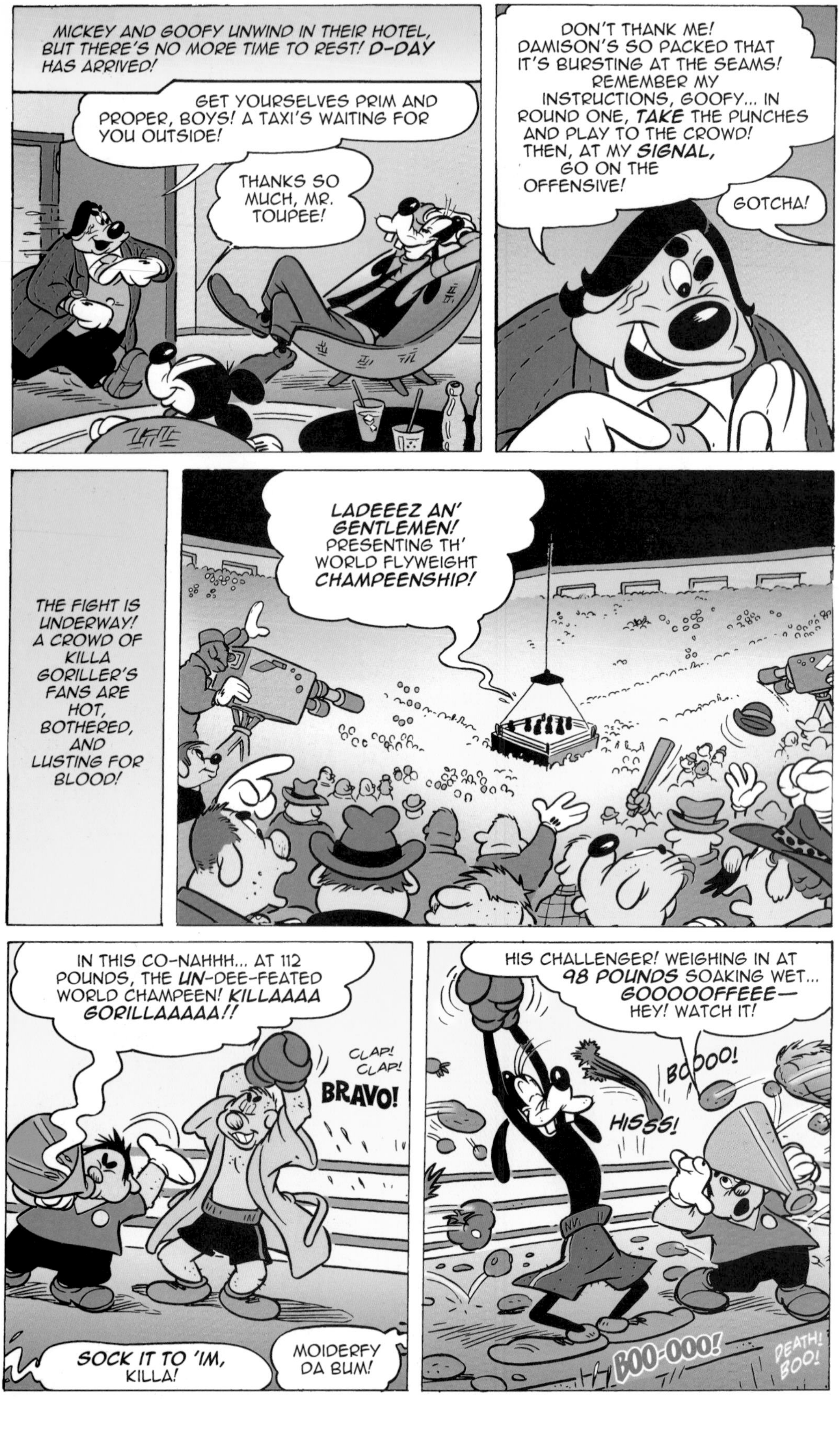
MICKEY AND GOOFY UNWIND IN THEIR HOTEL, BUT THERE'S NO MORE TIME TO REST! D-DAY HAS ARRIVED!
GET YOURSELVES PRIM AND PROPER, BOYS! A TAXI'S WAITING FOR YOU OUTSIDE!
THANKS SO MUCH, MR. TOUPEE!
DON'T THANK ME! DAMISON'S SO PACKED THAT IT'S BURSTING AT THE SEAMS!
REMEMBER MY INSTRUCTIONS, GOOFY... IN ROUND ONE, TAKE THE PUNCHES AND PLAY TO THE CROWD! THEN, AT MY SIGNAL, GO ON THE OFFENSIVE!
GOTCHA!
THE FIGHT IS UNDERWAY! A CROWD OF KILLA GORILLER'S FANS ARE HOT, BOTHERED, AND LUSTING FOR BLOOD!
LADEEEZ AN' GENTLEMEN! PRESENTING TH' WORLD FLYWEIGHT CHAMPEENSHIP!
IN THIS CO-NAHHH... AT 112 POUNDS, THE UN-DEE-FEATED WORLD CHAMPEEN! KILLAAAA GORILLAAAAA!!
CLAP! CLAP!
BRAVO!
SOCK IT TO 'IM, KILLA!
MOIDERFY DA BUM!
HIS CHALLENGER! WEIGHING IN AT 98 POUNDS SOAKING WET... GOOOOOFFEEE— HEY! WATCH IT!
BOOOO!
HISSS!
BOO-OOO!
DEATH! BOO!

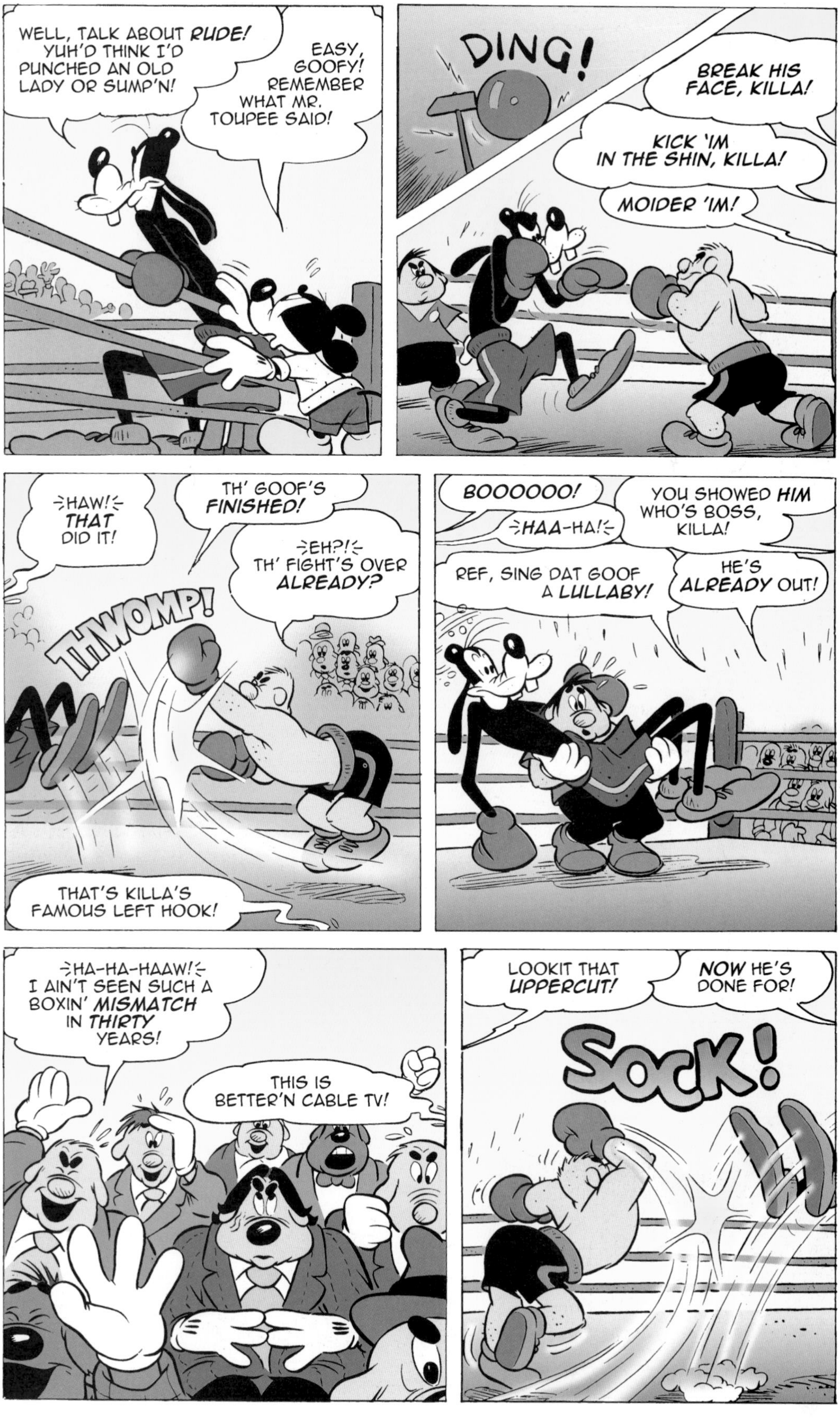
WELL, TALK ABOUT RUDE! YUH'D THINK I'D PUNCHED AN OLD LADY OR SUMP'N!
EASY, GOOFY! REMEMBER WHAT MR. TOUPEE SAID!
DING!
BREAK HIS FACE, KILLA!
KICK 'IM IN THE SHIN, KILLA!
MOIDER 'IM!
HAW! THAT DID IT!
TH' GOOF'S FINISHED!
EH?! TH' FIGHT'S OVER ALREADY?
THWOMP!
THAT'S KILLA'S FAMOUS LEFT HOOK!
BOOOOOO!
HAA-HA!
YOU SHOWED HIM WHO'S BOSS, KILLA!
REF, SING DAT GOOF A LULLABY!
HE'S ALREADY OUT!
HA-HA-HAAW! I AIN'T SEEN SUCH A BOXIN' MISMATCH IN THIRTY YEARS!
THIS IS BETTER'N CABLE TV!
LOOKIT THAT UPPERCUT!
NOW HE'S DONE FOR!
SOCK!

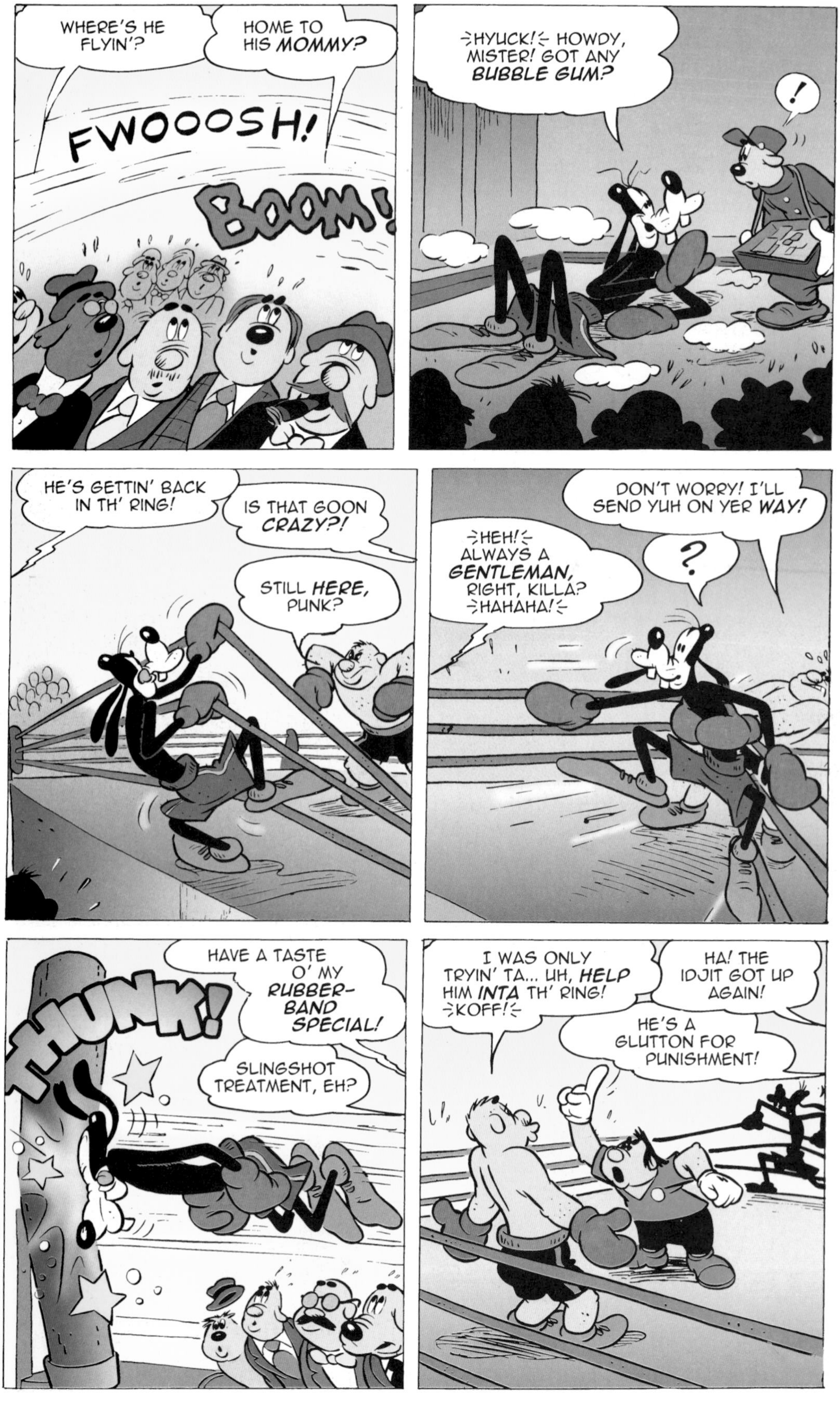
WHERE'S HE FLYIN'?
HOME TO HIS MOMMY?
FWOOOSH!
BOOM!
HYUCK! HOWDY, MISTER! GOT ANY BUBBLE GUM?
!
HE'S GETTIN' BACK IN TH' RING!
IS THAT GOON CRAZY?!
STILL HERE, PUNK?
DON'T WORRY! I'LL SEND YUH ON YER WAY!
HEH! ALWAYS A GENTLEMAN, RIGHT, KILLA? HAHAHA!
?
HAVE A TASTE O' MY RUBBER-BAND SPECIAL!
SLINGSHOT TREATMENT, EH?
THUNK!
I WAS ONLY TRYIN' TA... UH, HELP HIM INTA TH' RING! KOFF!
HA! THE IDJIT GOT UP AGAIN!
HE'S A GLUTTON FOR PUNISHMENT!

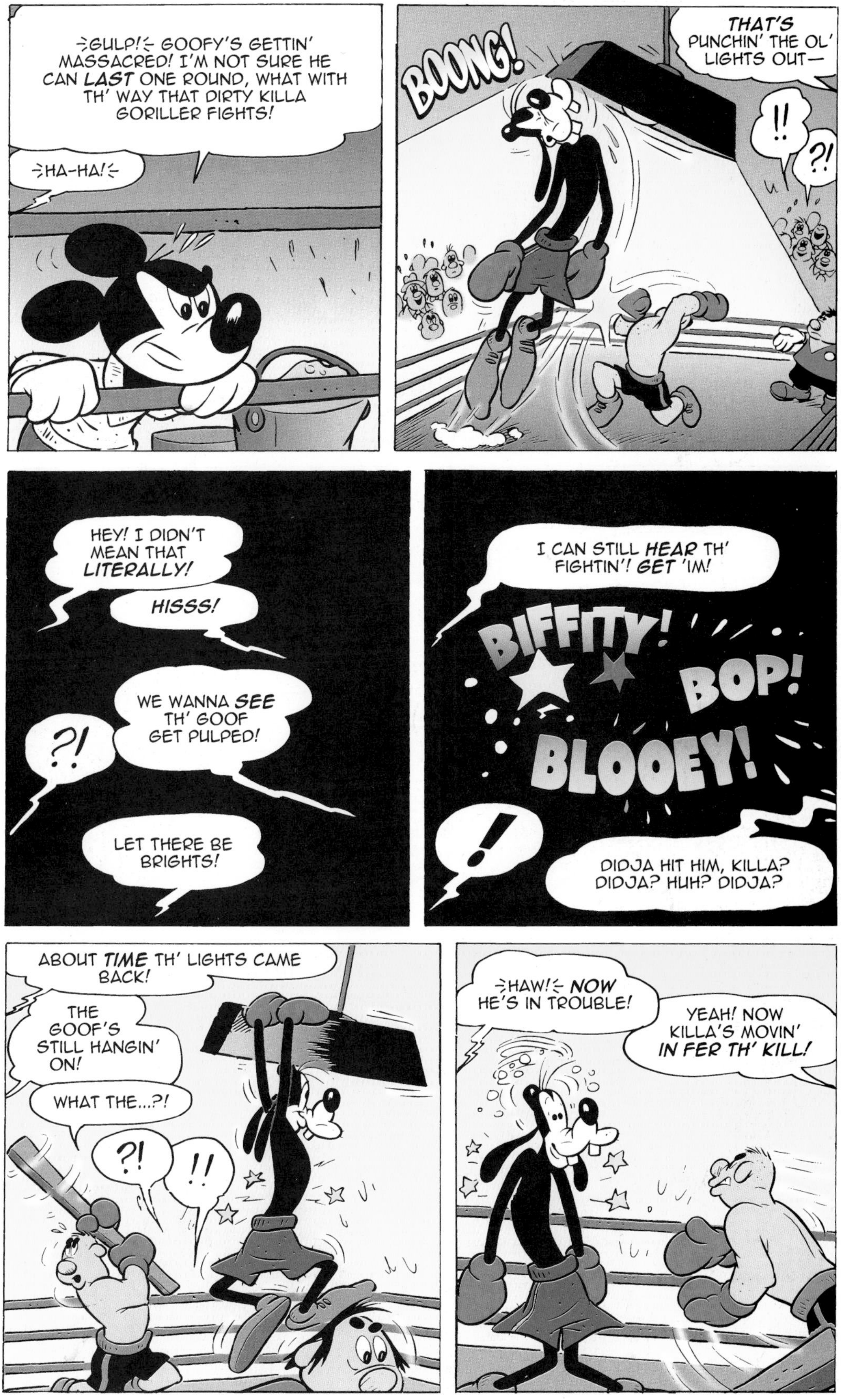
-GULP!- GOOFY'S GETTIN' MASSACRED! I'M NOT SURE HE CAN LAST ONE ROUND, WHAT WITH TH' WAY THAT DIRTY KILLA GORILLER FIGHTS!
-HA-HA!-
BOONG!
THAT'S PUNCHIN' THE OL' LIGHTS OUT—
!!
?!
HEY! I DIDN'T MEAN THAT LITERALLY!
HISSS!
WE WANNA SEE TH' GOOF GET PULPED!
?!
LET THERE BE BRIGHTS!
I CAN STILL HEAR TH' FIGHTIN'! GET 'IM!
BIFFITY!
BOP!
BLOOEY!
!
DIDJA HIT HIM, KILLA? DIDJA? HUH? DIDJA?
ABOUT TIME TH' LIGHTS CAME BACK!
THE GOOF'S STILL HANGIN' ON!
WHAT THE...?!
?!
!!
-HAW!- NOW HE'S IN TROUBLE!
YEAH! NOW KILLA'S MOVIN' IN FER TH' KILL!

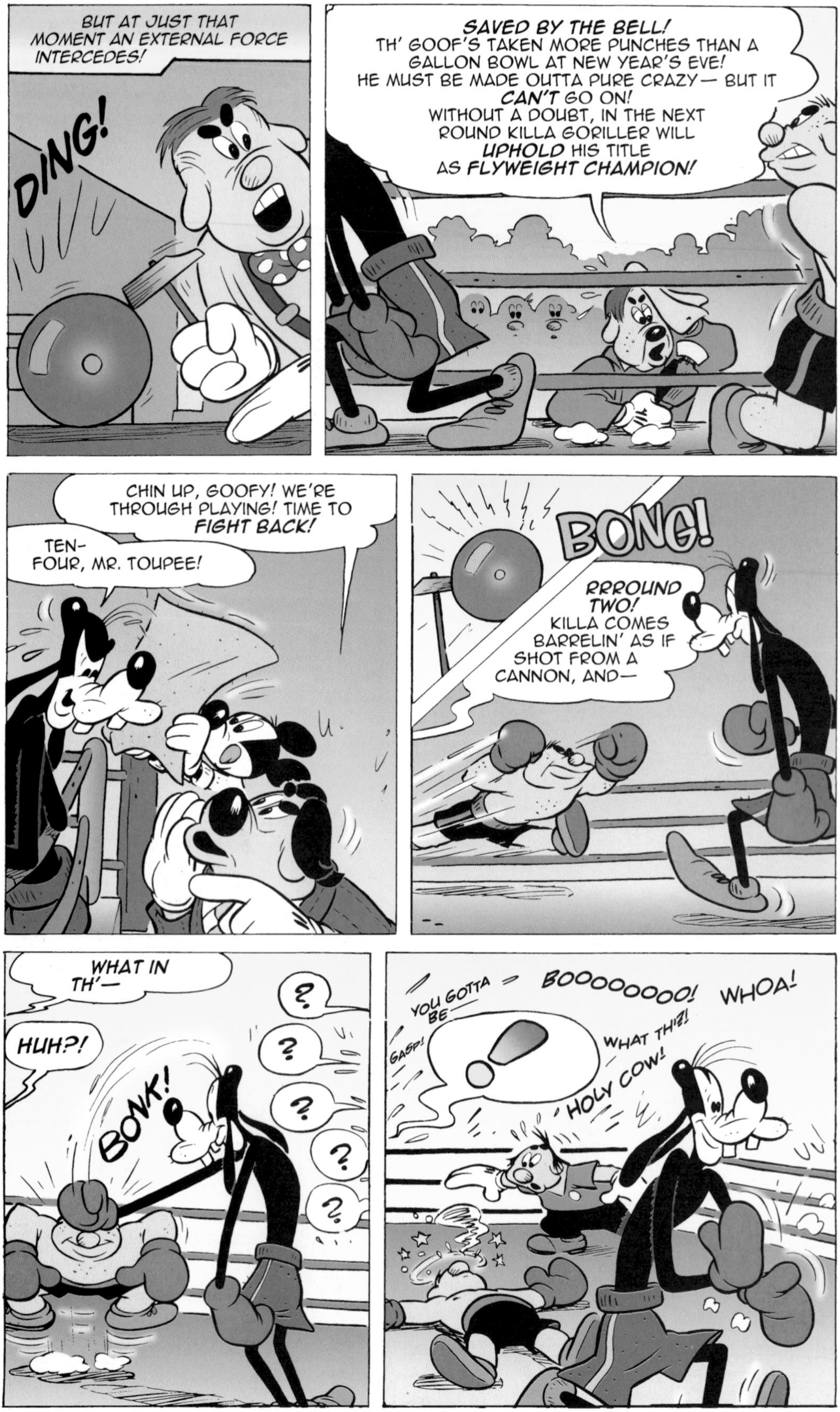

BUT AT JUST THAT MOMENT AN EXTERNAL FORCE INTERCEDES!
DING!
SAVED BY THE BELL!
TH' GOOF'S TAKEN MORE PUNCHES THAN A GALLON BOWL AT NEW YEAR'S EVE!
HE MUST BE MADE OUTTA PURE CRAZY— BUT IT CAN'T GO ON!
WITHOUT A DOUBT, IN THE NEXT ROUND KILLA GORILLER WILL UPHOLD HIS TITLE AS FLYWEIGHT CHAMPION!
CHIN UP, GOOFY! WE'RE THROUGH PLAYING! TIME TO FIGHT BACK!
TEN-FOUR, MR. TOUPEE!
BONG!
RRROUND TWO!
KILLA COMES BARRELIN' AS IF SHOT FROM A CANNON, AND—
WHAT IN TH'—
HUH?!
BONK!
?
?
?
?
?
YOU GOTTA BE—
BOOOOOOOO!
WHOA!
GASP!
!
WHAT TH'?!
HOLY COW!

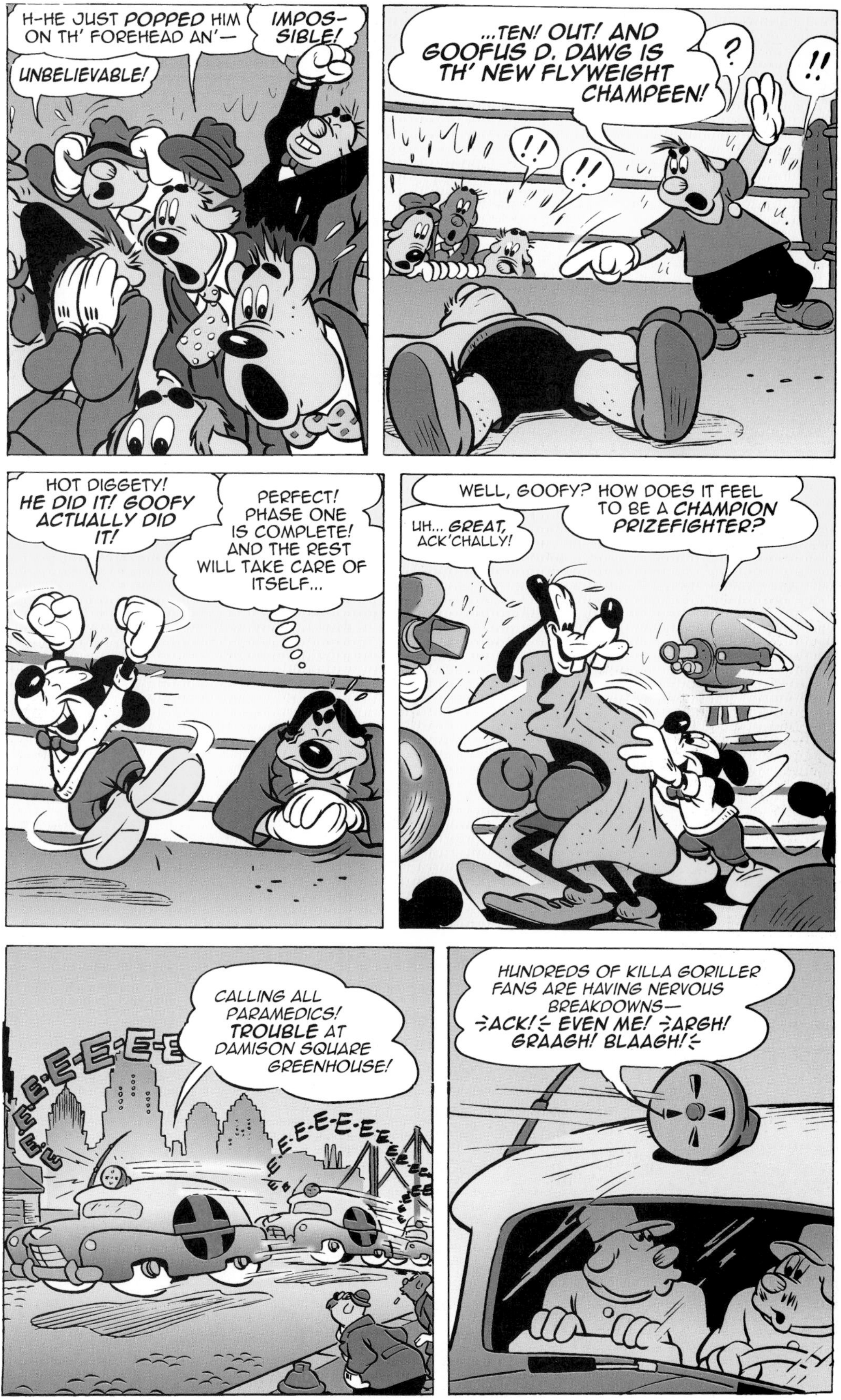
H-HE JUST POPPED HIM ON TH' FOREHEAD AN'—
IMPOS-SIBLE!
UNBELIEVABLE!
...TEN! OUT! AND GOOFUS D. DAWG IS TH' NEW FLYWEIGHT CHAMPEEN!
?
!!
!!
!!
HOT DIGGETY! HE DID IT! GOOFY ACTUALLY DID IT!
PERFECT! PHASE ONE IS COMPLETE! AND THE REST WILL TAKE CARE OF ITSELF...
WELL, GOOFY? HOW DOES IT FEEL TO BE A CHAMPION PRIZEFIGHTER?
UH... GREAT, ACK'CHALLY!
CALLING ALL PARAMEDICS! TROUBLE AT DAMISON SQUARE GREENHOUSE!
E-E-E-E-E-E-E-E-E
E-E-E-E-E-E-E-E-E-E-E-E
HUNDREDS OF KILLA GORILLER FANS ARE HAVING NERVOUS BREAKDOWNS—
ACK! EVEN ME! ARGH! GRAAGH! BLAAGH!

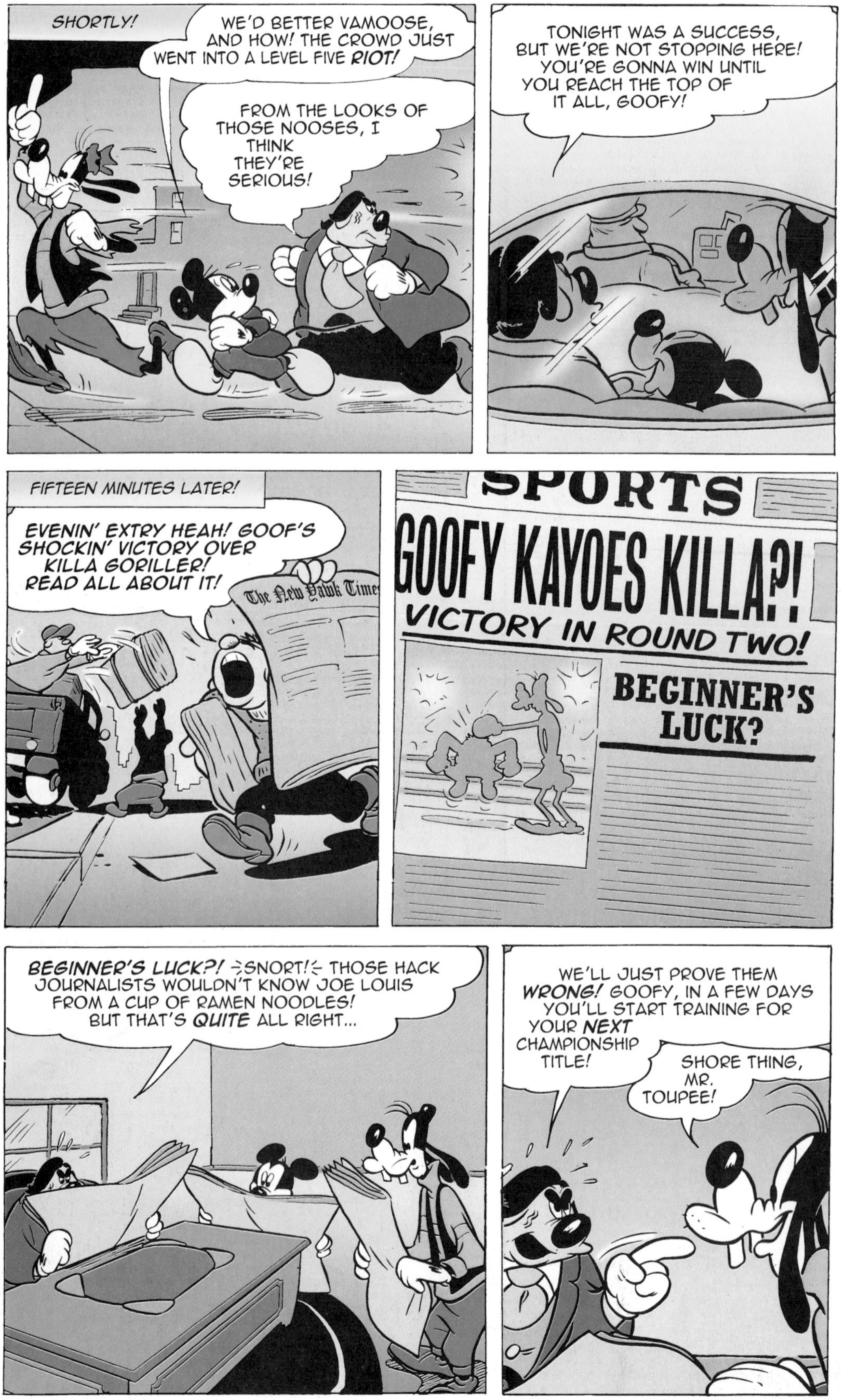
SHORTLY!
WE'D BETTER VAMOOSE, AND HOW! THE CROWD JUST WENT INTO A LEVEL FIVE RIOT!
FROM THE LOOKS OF THOSE NOOSES, I THINK THEY'RE SERIOUS!
TONIGHT WAS A SUCCESS, BUT WE'RE NOT STOPPING HERE! YOU'RE GONNA WIN UNTIL YOU REACH THE TOP OF IT ALL, GOOFY!
FIFTEEN MINUTES LATER!
EVENIN' EXTRY HEAH! GOOF'S SHOCKIN' VICTORY OVER KILLA GORILLER! READ ALL ABOUT IT!
The New Yawk Times
SPORTS
GOOFY KAYOES KILLA?!
VICTORY IN ROUND TWO!
BEGINNER'S LUCK?
BEGINNER'S LUCK?! -SNORT!- THOSE HACK JOURNALISTS WOULDN'T KNOW JOE LOUIS FROM A CUP OF RAMEN NOODLES! BUT THAT'S QUITE ALL RIGHT...
WE'LL JUST PROVE THEM WRONG! GOOFY, IN A FEW DAYS YOU'LL START TRAINING FOR YOUR NEXT CHAMPIONSHIP TITLE!
SHORE THING, MR. TOUPEE!

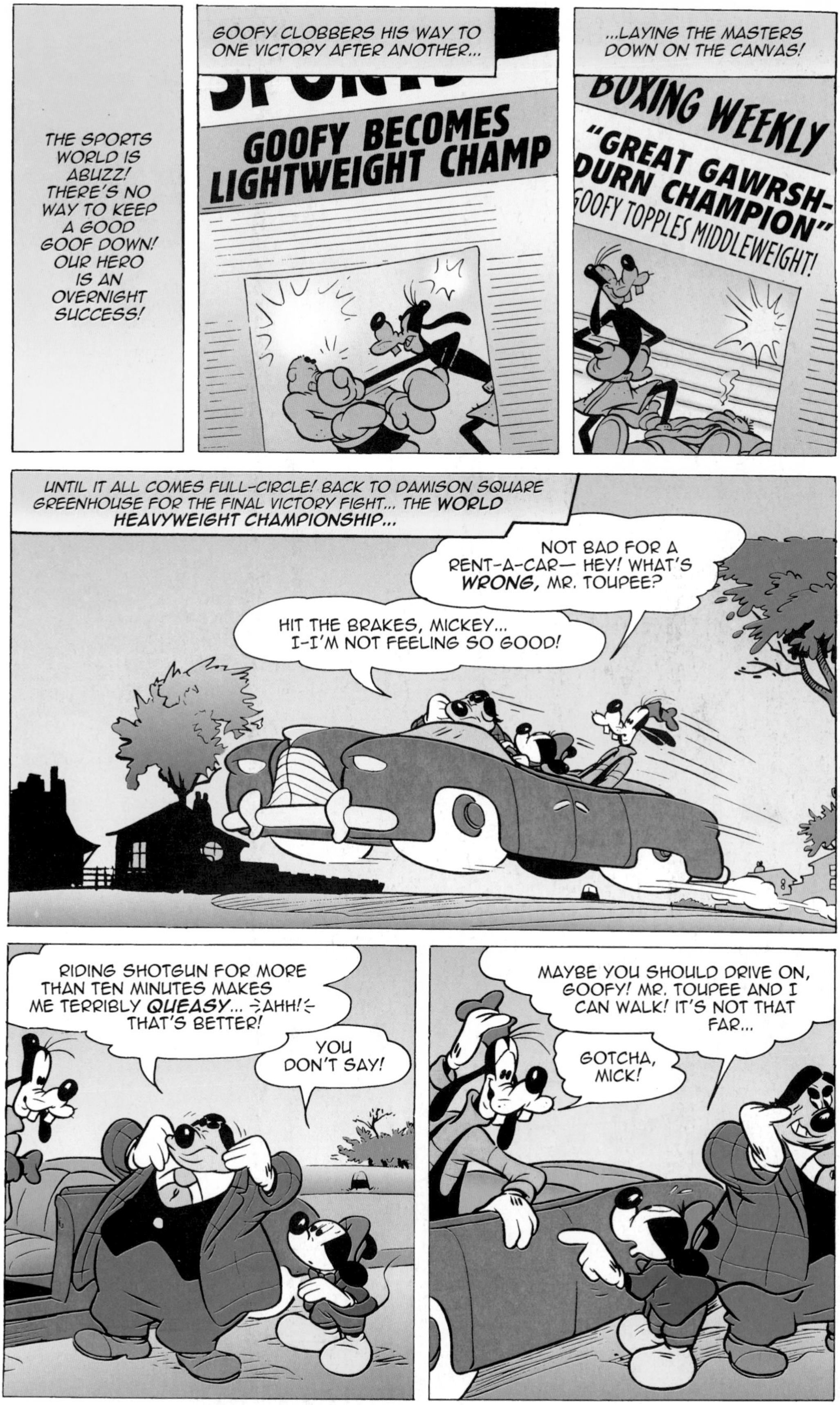
THE SPORTS WORLD IS ABUZZ! THERE'S NO WAY TO KEEP A GOOD GOOF DOWN! OUR HERO IS AN OVERNIGHT SUCCESS!
GOOFY CLOBBERS HIS WAY TO ONE VICTORY AFTER ANOTHER...
GOOFY BECOMES LIGHTWEIGHT CHAMP
...LAYING THE MASTERS DOWN ON THE CANVAS!
BOXING WEEKLY
"GREAT GAWRSH-DURN CHAMPION"
GOOFY TOPPLES MIDDLEWEIGHT!
UNTIL IT ALL COMES FULL-CIRCLE! BACK TO DAMISON SQUARE GREENHOUSE FOR THE FINAL VICTORY FIGHT... THE WORLD HEAVYWEIGHT CHAMPIONSHIP...
NOT BAD FOR A RENT-A-CAR— HEY! WHAT'S WRONG, MR. TOUPEE?
HIT THE BRAKES, MICKEY... I-I'M NOT FEELING SO GOOD!
RIDING SHOTGUN FOR MORE THAN TEN MINUTES MAKES ME TERRIBLY QUEASY... AHH! THAT'S BETTER!
YOU DON'T SAY!
MAYBE YOU SHOULD DRIVE ON, GOOFY! MR. TOUPEE AND I CAN WALK! IT'S NOT THAT FAR...
GOTCHA, MICK!

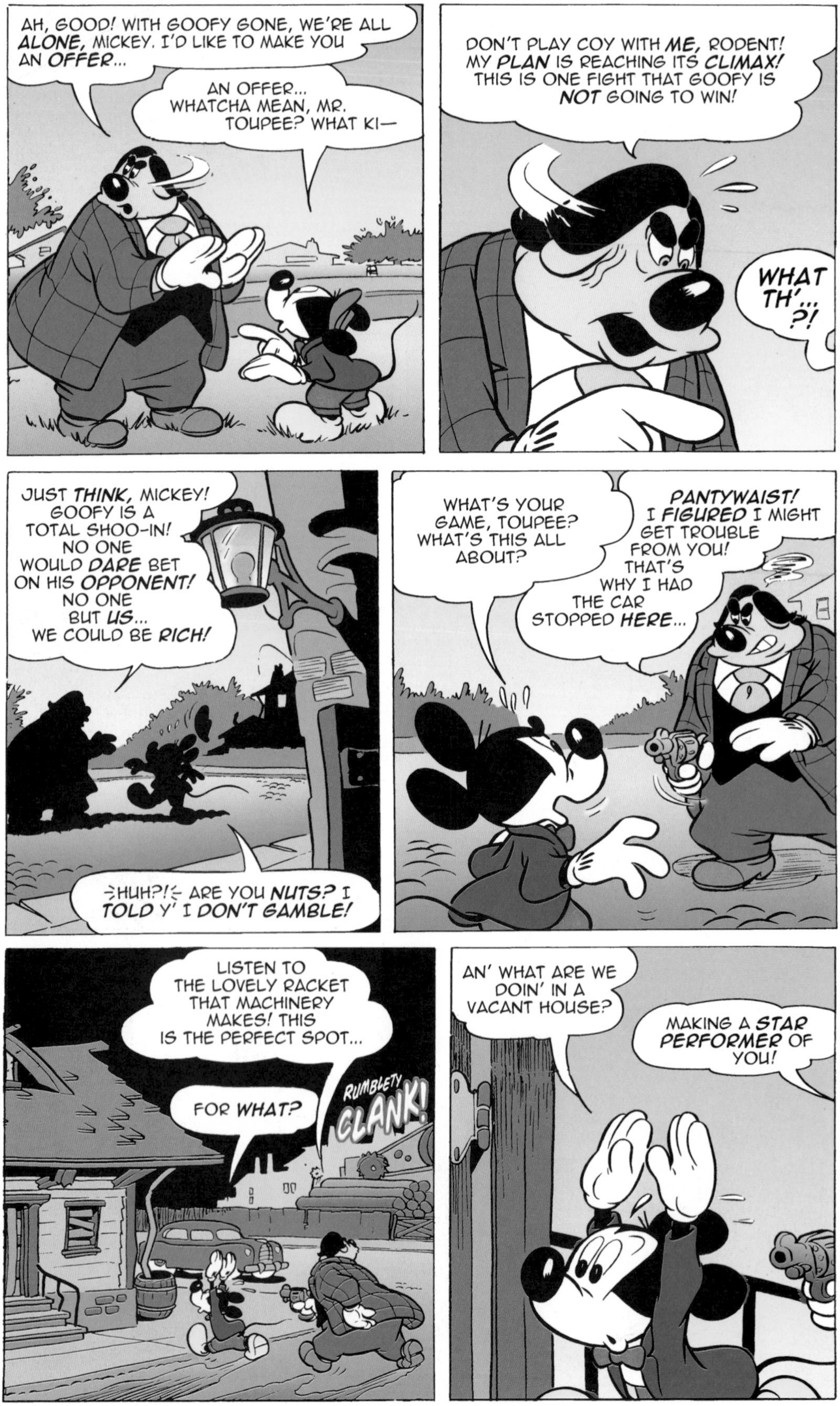
AH, GOOD! WITH GOOFY GONE, WE'RE ALL ALONE, MICKEY. I'D LIKE TO MAKE YOU AN OFFER...
AN OFFER... WHATCHA MEAN, MR. TOUPEE? WHAT KI—
DON'T PLAY COY WITH ME, RODENT! MY PLAN IS REACHING ITS CLIMAX! THIS IS ONE FIGHT THAT GOOFY IS NOT GOING TO WIN!
WHAT TH'...?!
JUST THINK, MICKEY! GOOFY IS A TOTAL SHOO-IN! NO ONE WOULD DARE BET ON HIS OPPONENT! NO ONE BUT US... WE COULD BE RICH!
HUH?! ARE YOU NUTS? I TOLD Y' I DON'T GAMBLE!
WHAT'S YOUR GAME, TOUPEE? WHAT'S THIS ALL ABOUT?
PANTYWAIST! I FIGURED I MIGHT GET TROUBLE FROM YOU! THAT'S WHY I HAD THE CAR STOPPED HERE...
LISTEN TO THE LOVELY RACKET THAT MACHINERY MAKES! THIS IS THE PERFECT SPOT...
FOR WHAT?
RUMBLETY CLANK!
AN' WHAT ARE WE DOIN' IN A VACANT HOUSE?
MAKING A STAR PERFORMER OF YOU!

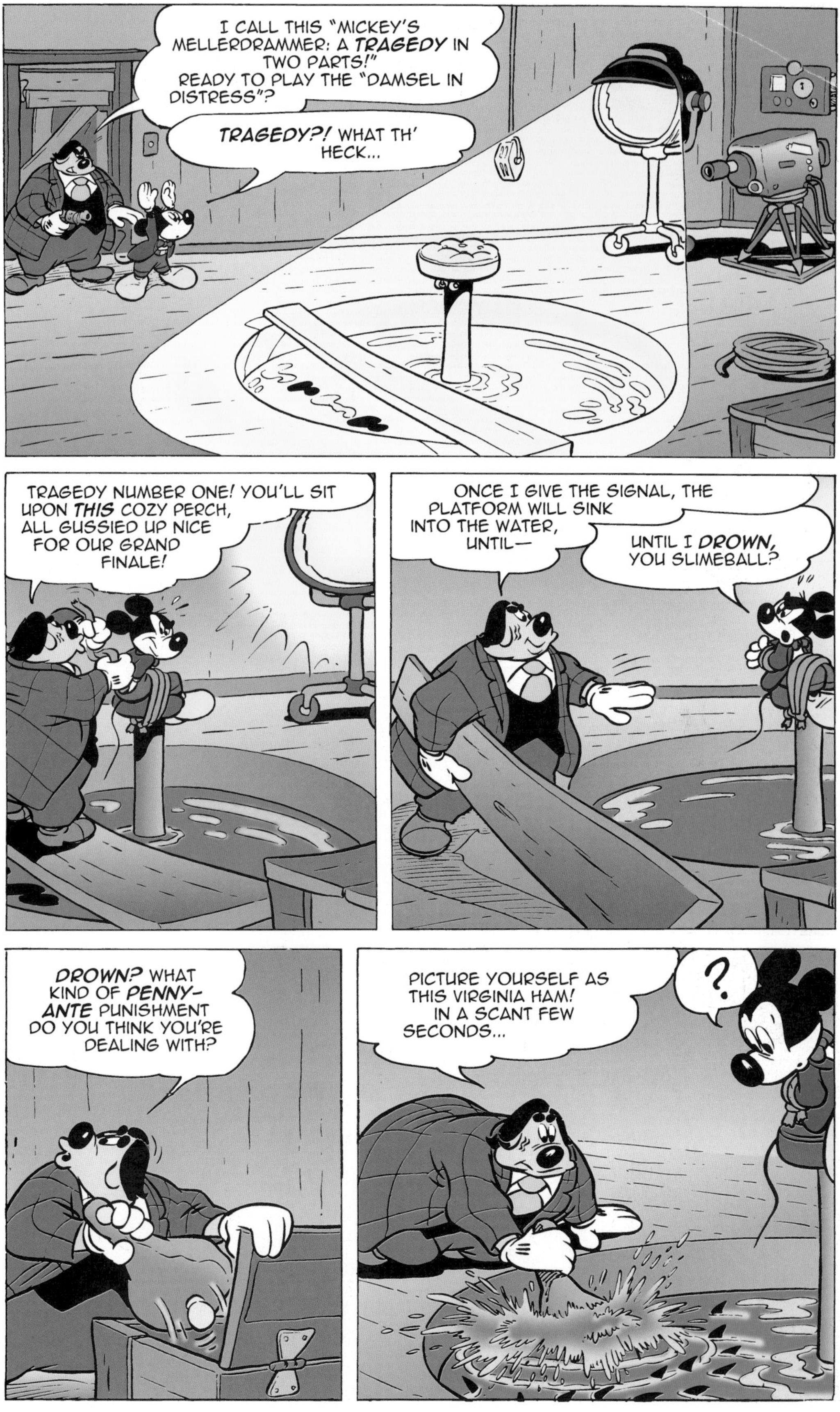
I CALL THIS "MICKEY'S MELLERDRAMMER: A *TRAGEDY* IN TWO PARTS!" READY TO PLAY THE "DAMSEL IN DISTRESS"?
TRAGEDY?! WHAT TH' HECK...
TRAGEDY NUMBER ONE! YOU'LL SIT UPON *THIS* COZY PERCH, ALL GUSSIED UP NICE FOR OUR GRAND FINALE!
ONCE I GIVE THE SIGNAL, THE PLATFORM WILL SINK INTO THE WATER, UNTIL—
UNTIL I *DROWN,* YOU SLIMEBALL?
DROWN? WHAT KIND OF *PENNY-ANTE* PUNISHMENT DO YOU THINK YOU'RE DEALING WITH?
PICTURE YOURSELF AS THIS VIRGINIA HAM! IN A SCANT FEW SECONDS...
?

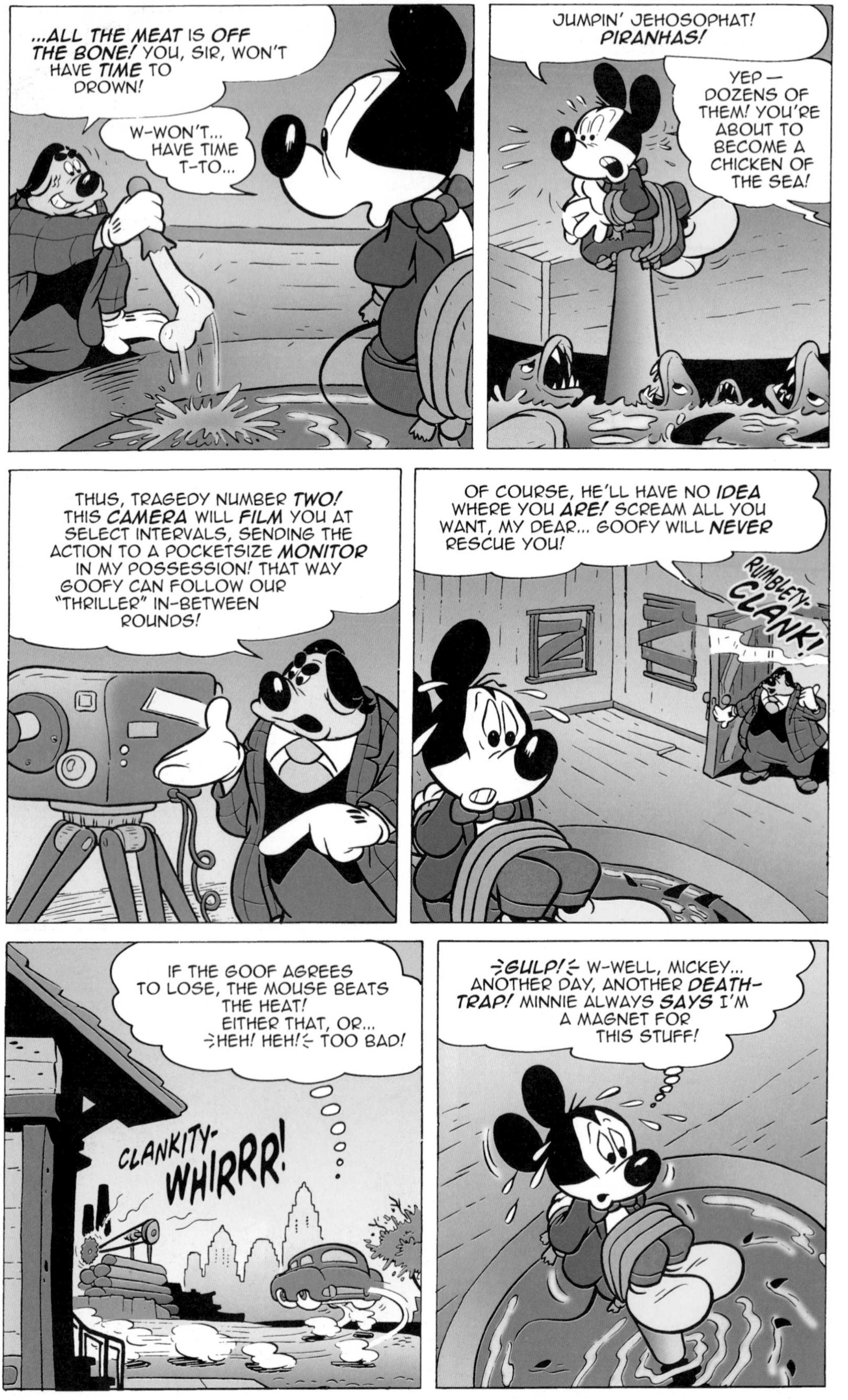
...ALL THE MEAT IS OFF THE BONE! YOU, SIR, WON'T HAVE TIME TO DROWN!
W-WON'T... HAVE TIME T-TO...
JUMPIN' JEHOSOPHAT! PIRANHAS!
YEP — DOZENS OF THEM! YOU'RE ABOUT TO BECOME A CHICKEN OF THE SEA!
THUS, TRAGEDY NUMBER TWO! THIS CAMERA WILL FILM YOU AT SELECT INTERVALS, SENDING THE ACTION TO A POCKETSIZE MONITOR IN MY POSSESSION! THAT WAY GOOFY CAN FOLLOW OUR "THRILLER" IN-BETWEEN ROUNDS!
OF COURSE, HE'LL HAVE NO IDEA WHERE YOU ARE! SCREAM ALL YOU WANT, MY DEAR... GOOFY WILL NEVER RESCUE YOU!
RUMBLETY-CLANK!
IF THE GOOF AGREES TO LOSE, THE MOUSE BEATS THE HEAT! EITHER THAT, OR... HEH! HEH! TOO BAD!
CLANKITY-WHIRRR!
GULP! W-WELL, MICKEY... ANOTHER DAY, ANOTHER DEATH-TRAP! MINNIE ALWAYS SAYS I'M A MAGNET FOR THIS STUFF!

I'VE ONLY GOT *MINUTES* TO DOPE OUT AN ESCAPE PLAN! MAYBE THERE'S *ONE* CHANCE... IF ONLY THESE DOGGONE FISH—

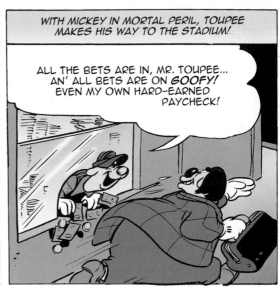

WITH MICKEY IN MORTAL PERIL, TOUPEE MAKES HIS WAY TO THE STADIUM!

ALL THE BETS ARE IN, MR. TOUPEE... AN' ALL BETS ARE ON *GOOFY!* EVEN MY OWN HARD-EARNED PAYCHECK!

THE FIGHT STARTS IN FIFTEEN MINUTES! THAT'S JUST ENOUGH TIME TO BREAK THE NEWS TO TALL, DARK AND CLUELESS!

HIYA, MR. TOUPEE! YUH FINALLY MADE IT... WHERE'S *MICKEY?*

SETTLE DOWN! HE'S COMING! BUT LISTEN...

HE AND I HAVE DECIDED YOU SHOULD *LOSE* THIS FIGHT! GET IT? ACK-BAY ON THE ANVAS-CAY!

SHURE! I— ⸮HUH?!⸰ WHUT'S *THAT* YER SAYIN'?

LOSE!?! BUT I *NEVER* LOSE! WHUT'S THUH IDEAR, PAL? I MAY BE A GOOF, BUT I AIN'T *STUPID!*

DON'T YOU QUESTION ME! *DO* AS I SAY!

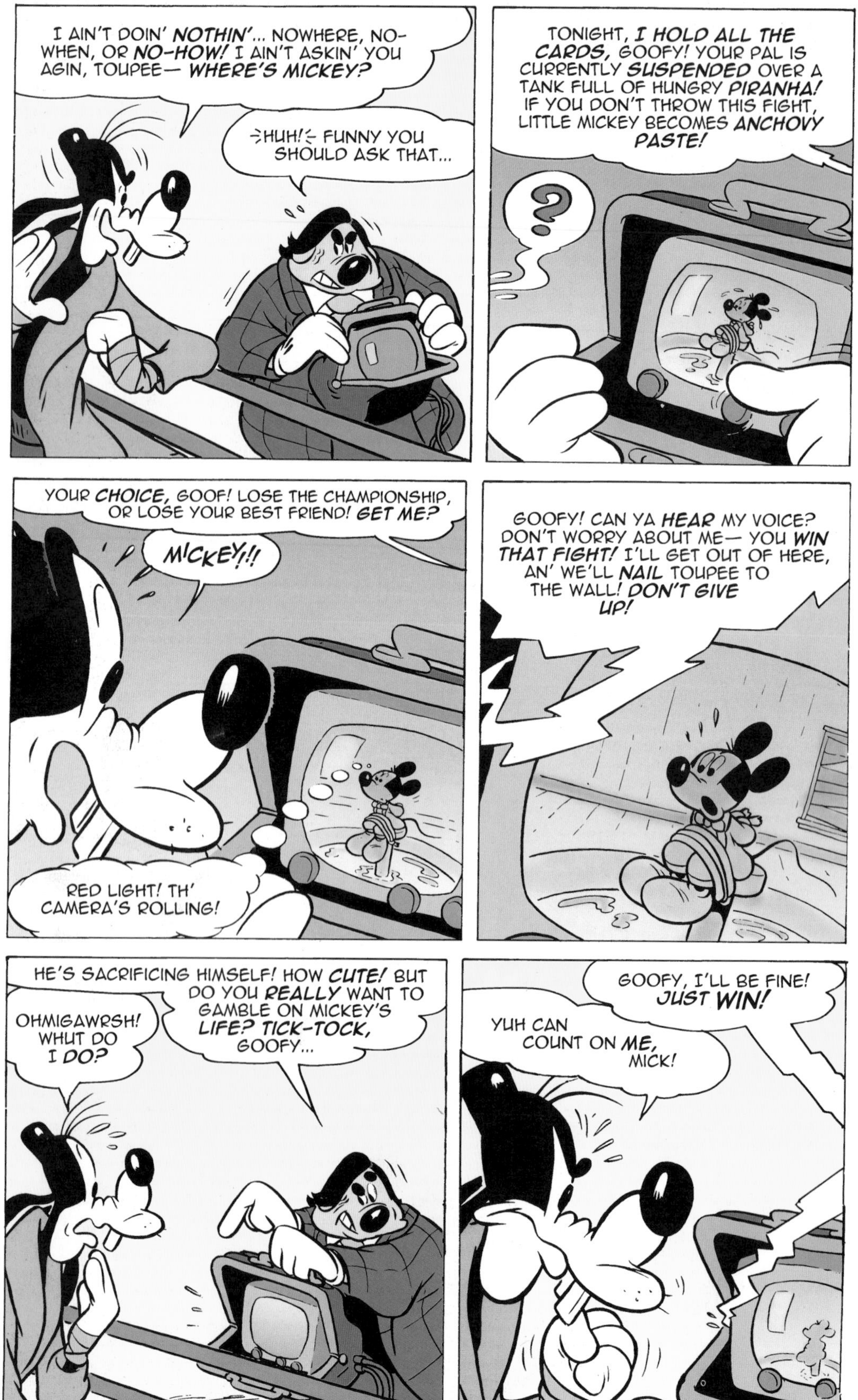

I AIN'T DOIN' NOTHIN'... NOWHERE, NO-WHEN, OR NO-HOW! I AIN'T ASKIN' YOU AGIN, TOUPEE— WHERE'S MICKEY?
HUH! FUNNY YOU SHOULD ASK THAT...
TONIGHT, I HOLD ALL THE CARDS, GOOFY! YOUR PAL IS CURRENTLY SUSPENDED OVER A TANK FULL OF HUNGRY PIRANHA! IF YOU DON'T THROW THIS FIGHT, LITTLE MICKEY BECOMES ANCHOVY PASTE!
?
YOUR CHOICE, GOOF! LOSE THE CHAMPIONSHIP, OR LOSE YOUR BEST FRIEND! GET ME?
MICKEY!!!
RED LIGHT! TH' CAMERA'S ROLLING!
GOOFY! CAN YA HEAR MY VOICE? DON'T WORRY ABOUT ME— YOU WIN THAT FIGHT! I'LL GET OUT OF HERE, AN' WE'LL NAIL TOUPEE TO THE WALL! DON'T GIVE UP!
HE'S SACRIFICING HIMSELF! HOW CUTE! BUT DO YOU REALLY WANT TO GAMBLE ON MICKEY'S LIFE? TICK-TOCK, GOOFY...
OHMIGAWRSH! WHUT DO I DO?
GOOFY, I'LL BE FINE! JUST WIN!
YUH CAN COUNT ON ME, MICK!

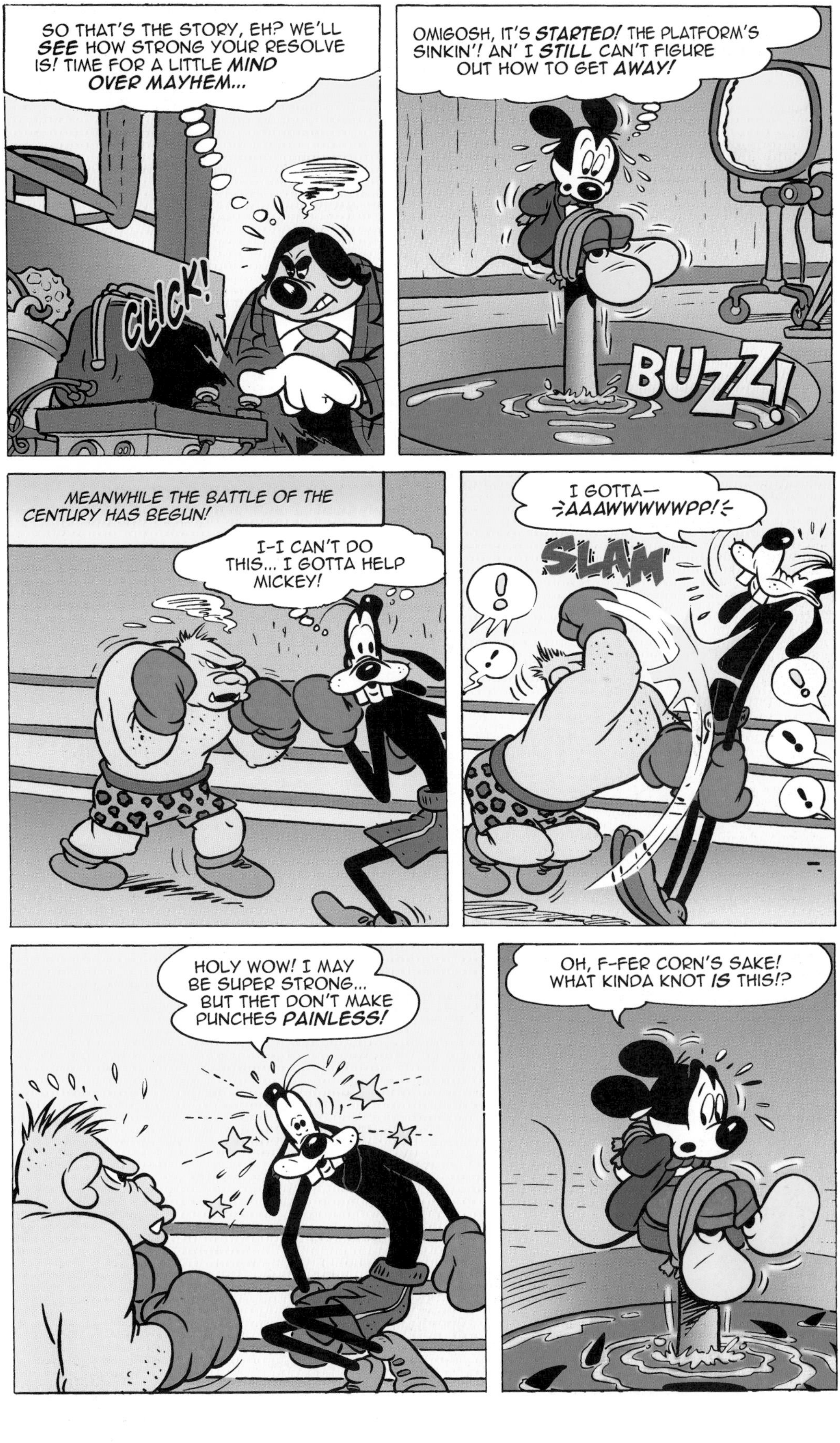
SO THAT'S THE STORY, EH? WE'LL SEE HOW STRONG YOUR RESOLVE IS! TIME FOR A LITTLE MIND OVER MAYHEM...
CLICK!
OMIGOSH, IT'S STARTED! THE PLATFORM'S SINKIN'! AN' I STILL CAN'T FIGURE OUT HOW TO GET AWAY!
BUZZ!
MEANWHILE THE BATTLE OF THE CENTURY HAS BEGUN!
I-I CAN'T DO THIS... I GOTTA HELP MICKEY!
I GOTTA—AAAWWWWWPP!
SLAM
!
!
!
!
!
HOLY WOW! I MAY BE SUPER STRONG... BUT THET DON'T MAKE PUNCHES PAINLESS!
OH, F-FER CORN'S SAKE! WHAT KINDA KNOT IS THIS!?

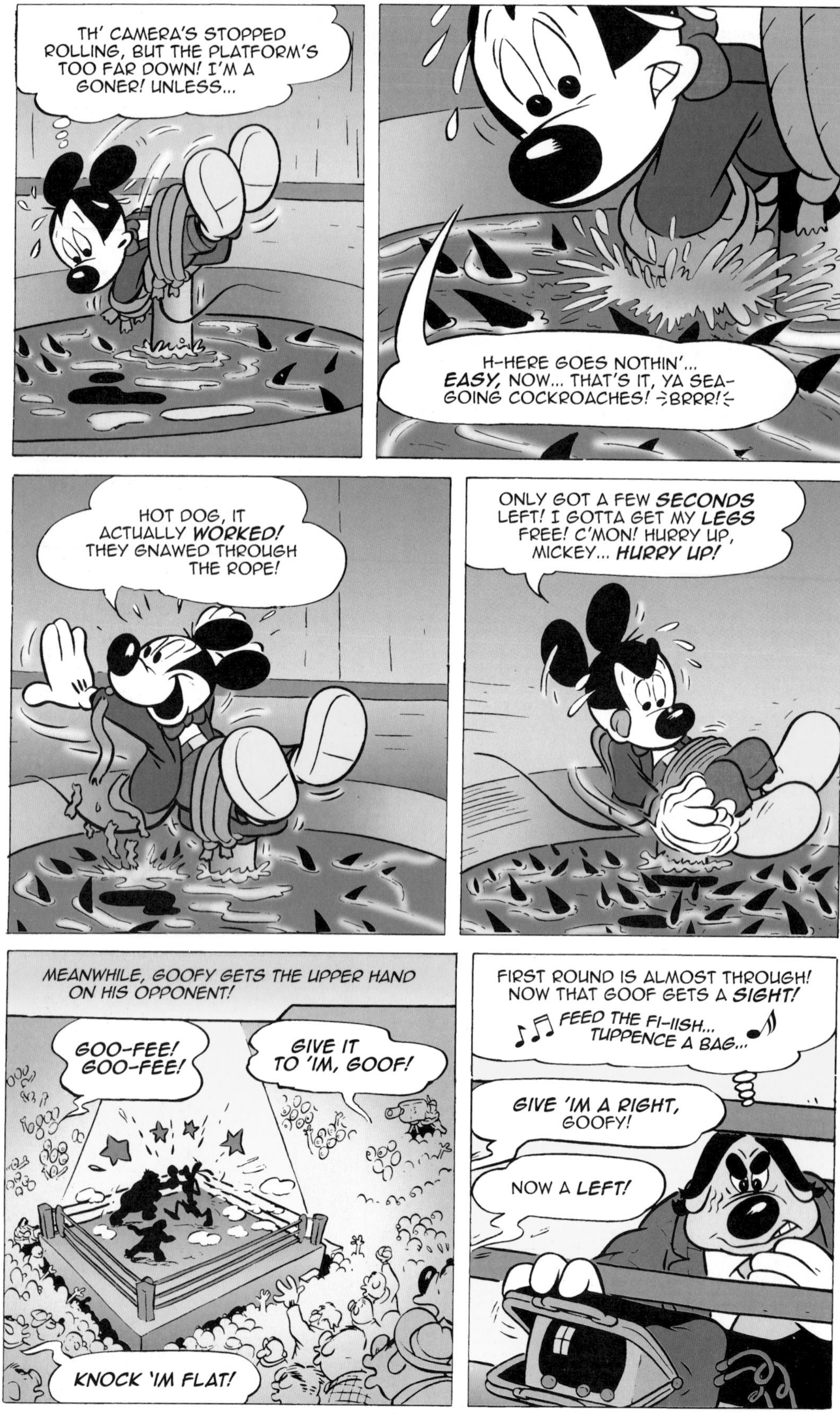

TH' CAMERA'S STOPPED ROLLING, BUT THE PLATFORM'S TOO FAR DOWN! I'M A GONER! UNLESS...
H-HERE GOES NOTHIN'... EASY, NOW... THAT'S IT, YA SEA-GOING COCKROACHES! BRRR!
HOT DOG, IT ACTUALLY WORKED! THEY GNAWED THROUGH THE ROPE!
ONLY GOT A FEW SECONDS LEFT! I GOTTA GET MY LEGS FREE! C'MON! HURRY UP, MICKEY... HURRY UP!
MEANWHILE, GOOFY GETS THE UPPER HAND ON HIS OPPONENT!
GOO-FEE! GOO-FEE!
GIVE IT TO 'IM, GOOF!
KNOCK 'IM FLAT!
FIRST ROUND IS ALMOST THROUGH! NOW THAT GOOF GETS A SIGHT!
FEED THE FI-IISH... TUPPENCE A BAG...
GIVE 'IM A RIGHT, GOOFY!
NOW A LEFT!

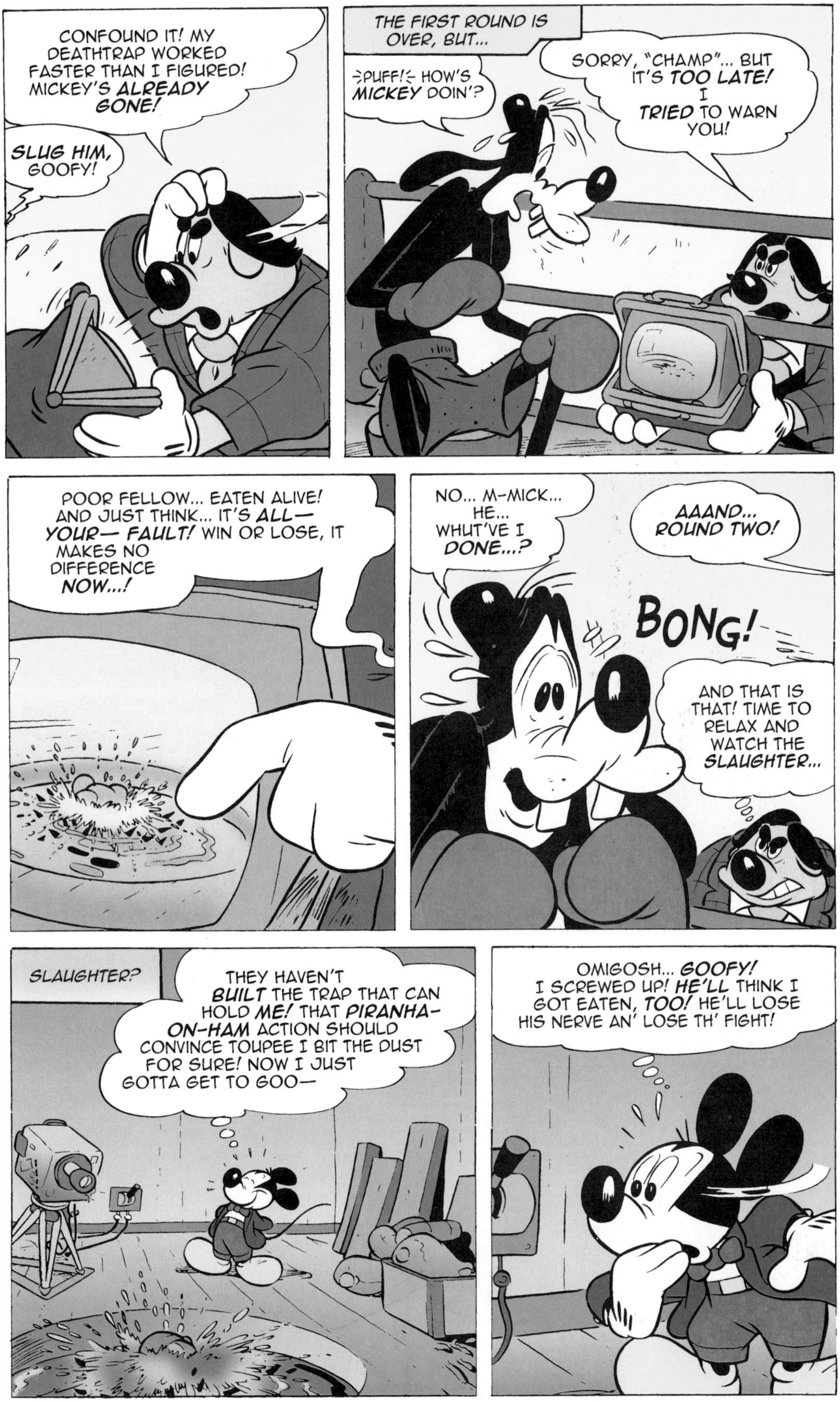
CONFOUND IT! MY DEATHTRAP WORKED FASTER THAN I FIGURED! MICKEY'S ALREADY GONE!
SLUG HIM, GOOFY!
THE FIRST ROUND IS OVER, BUT...
PUFF! HOW'S MICKEY DOIN'?
SORRY, "CHAMP"... BUT IT'S TOO LATE! I TRIED TO WARN YOU!
POOR FELLOW... EATEN ALIVE! AND JUST THINK... IT'S ALL— YOUR— FAULT! WIN OR LOSE, IT MAKES NO DIFFERENCE NOW...!
NO... M-MICK... HE... WHUT'VE I DONE...?
AAAND... ROUND TWO!
BONG!
AND THAT IS THAT! TIME TO RELAX AND WATCH THE SLAUGHTER...
SLAUGHTER?
THEY HAVEN'T BUILT THE TRAP THAT CAN HOLD ME! THAT PIRANHA-ON-HAM ACTION SHOULD CONVINCE TOUPEE I BIT THE DUST FOR SURE! NOW I JUST GOTTA GET TO GOO—
OMIGOSH... GOOFY! I SCREWED UP! HE'LL THINK I GOT EATEN, TOO! HE'LL LOSE HIS NERVE AN' LOSE TH' FIGHT!

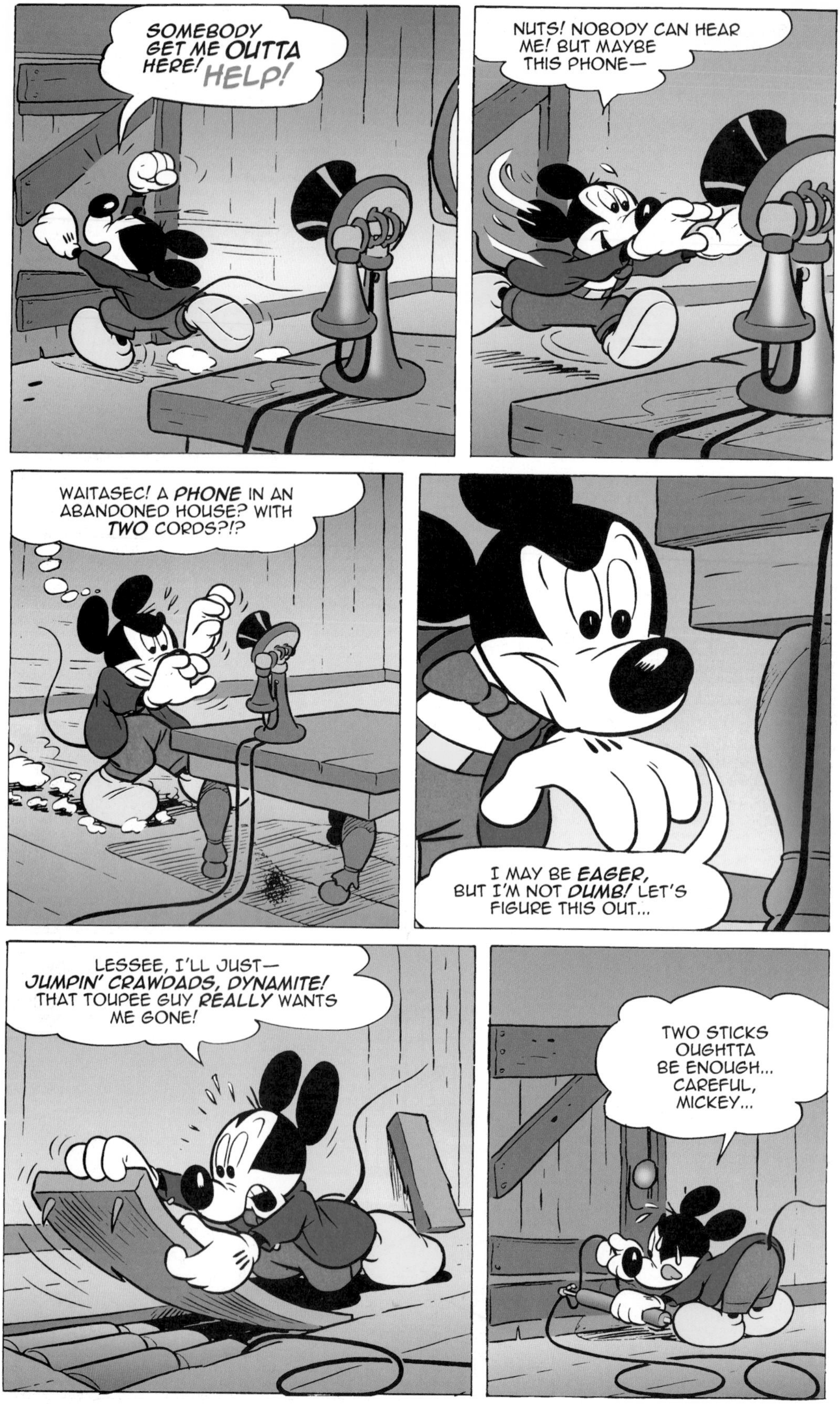
SOMEBODY GET ME OUTTA HERE! HELP!
NUTS! NOBODY CAN HEAR ME! BUT MAYBE THIS PHONE—
WAITASEC! A PHONE IN AN ABANDONED HOUSE? WITH TWO CORDS?!?
I MAY BE EAGER, BUT I'M NOT DUMB! LET'S FIGURE THIS OUT...
LESSEE, I'LL JUST— JUMPIN' CRAWDADS, DYNAMITE! THAT TOUPEE GUY REALLY WANTS ME GONE!
TWO STICKS OUGHTTA BE ENOUGH... CAREFUL, MICKEY...

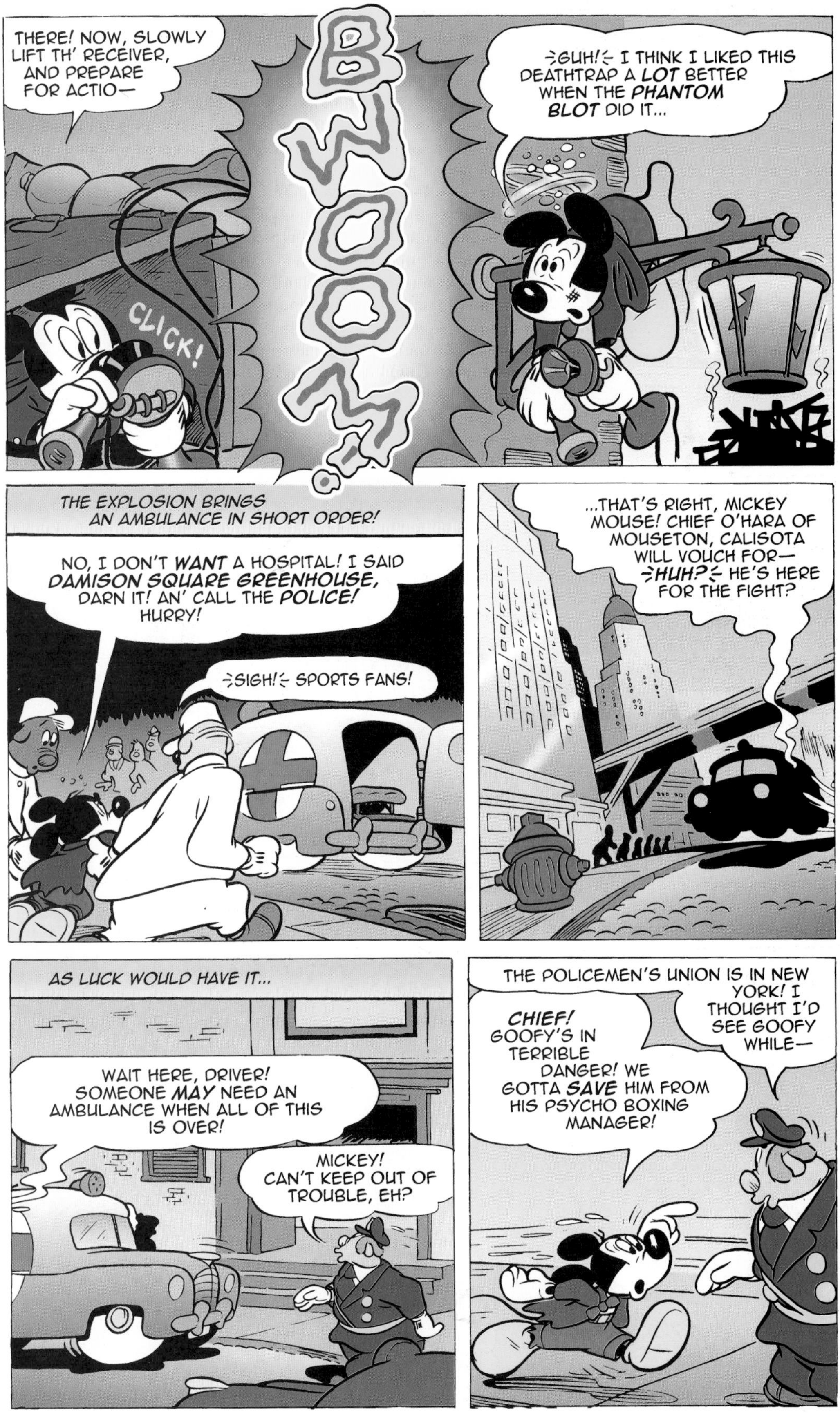
THERE! NOW, SLOWLY LIFT TH' RECEIVER, AND PREPARE FOR ACTIO—
CLICK!
BWOOM!
-GUH!- I THINK I LIKED THIS DEATHTRAP A LOT BETTER WHEN THE PHANTOM BLOT DID IT...
THE EXPLOSION BRINGS AN AMBULANCE IN SHORT ORDER!
NO, I DON'T WANT A HOSPITAL! I SAID DAMISON SQUARE GREENHOUSE, DARN IT! AN' CALL THE POLICE! HURRY!
-SIGH!- SPORTS FANS!
...THAT'S RIGHT, MICKEY MOUSE! CHIEF O'HARA OF MOUSETON, CALISOTA WILL VOUCH FOR— -HUH?- HE'S HERE FOR THE FIGHT?
AS LUCK WOULD HAVE IT...
WAIT HERE, DRIVER! SOMEONE MAY NEED AN AMBULANCE WHEN ALL OF THIS IS OVER!
MICKEY! CAN'T KEEP OUT OF TROUBLE, EH?
THE POLICEMEN'S UNION IS IN NEW YORK! I THOUGHT I'D SEE GOOFY WHILE—
CHIEF! GOOFY'S IN TERRIBLE DANGER! WE GOTTA SAVE HIM FROM HIS PSYCHO BOXING MANAGER!

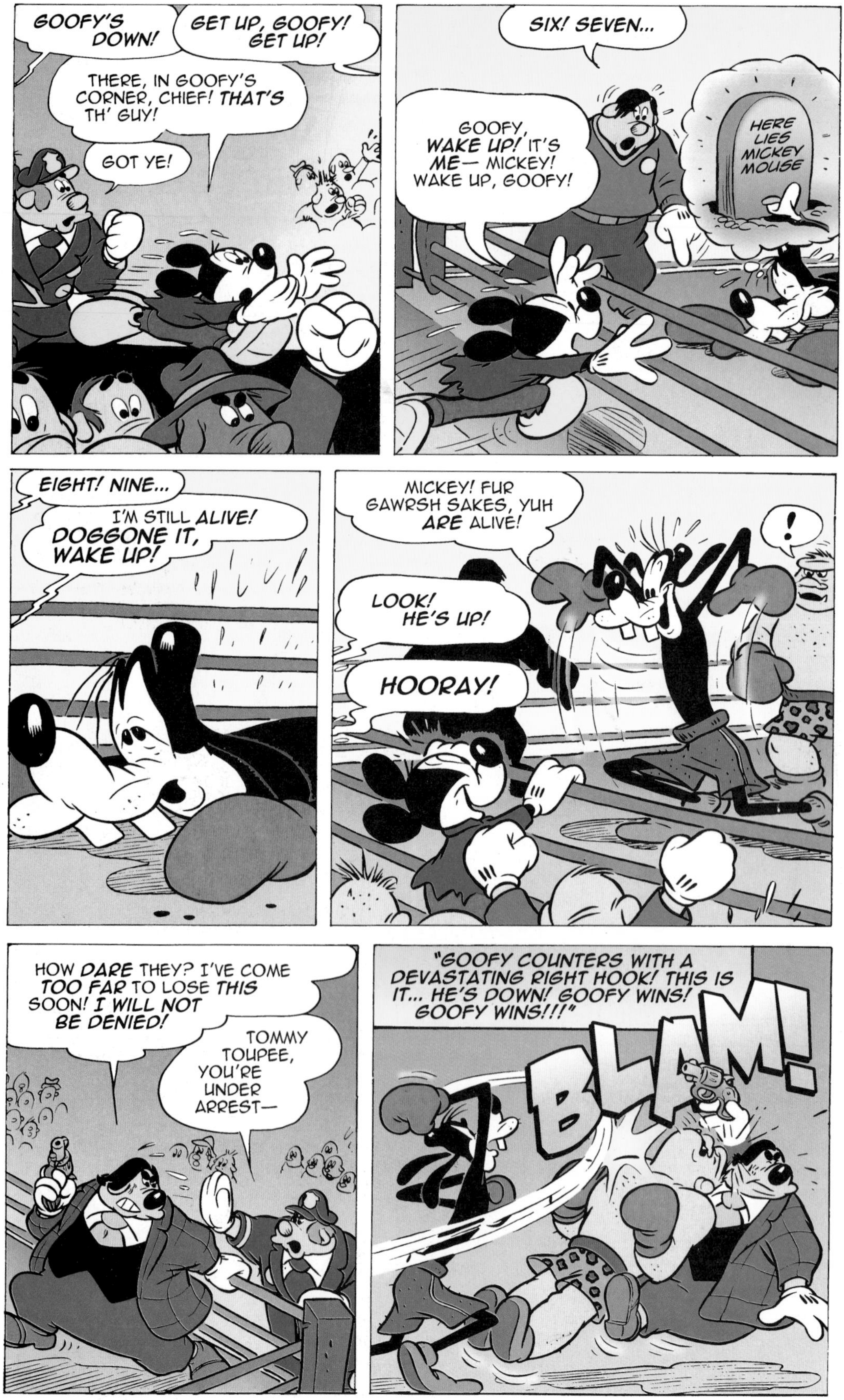
GOOFY'S DOWN!
GET UP, GOOFY! GET UP!
THERE, IN GOOFY'S CORNER, CHIEF! THAT'S TH' GUY!
GOT YE!
SIX! SEVEN...
GOOFY, WAKE UP! IT'S ME— MICKEY! WAKE UP, GOOFY!
HERE LIES MICKEY MOUSE
EIGHT! NINE...
I'M STILL ALIVE! DOGGONE IT, WAKE UP!
MICKEY! FUR GAWRSH SAKES, YUH ARE ALIVE!
!
LOOK! HE'S UP!
HOORAY!
HOW DARE THEY? I'VE COME TOO FAR TO LOSE THIS SOON! I WILL NOT BE DENIED!
TOMMY TOUPEE, YOU'RE UNDER ARREST—
"GOOFY COUNTERS WITH A DEVASTATING RIGHT HOOK! THIS IS IT... HE'S DOWN! GOOFY WINS! GOOFY WINS!!!"
BLAM!

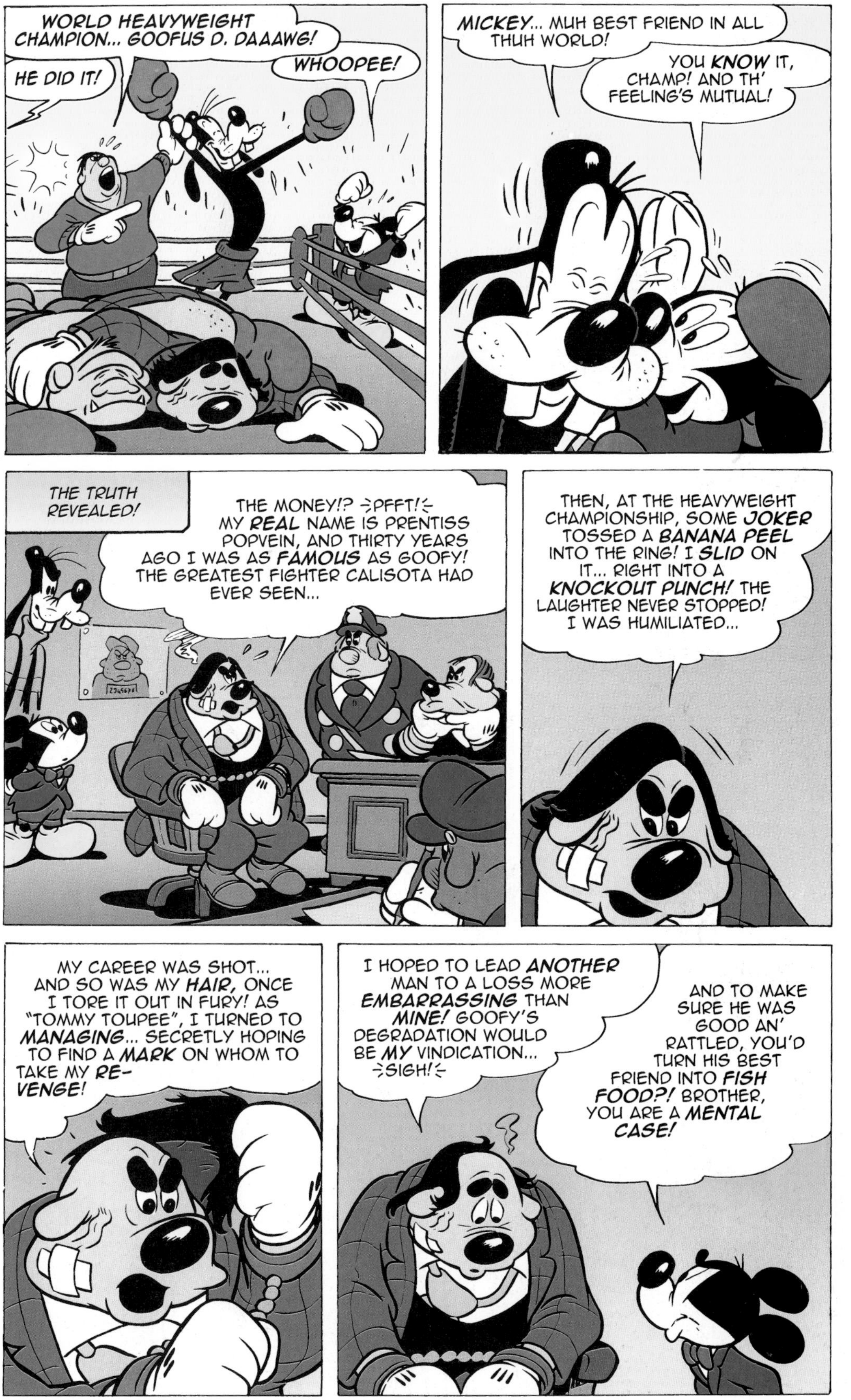
WORLD HEAVYWEIGHT CHAMPION... GOOFUS D. DAAAWG!
HE DID IT!
WHOOPEE!
MICKEY... MUH BEST FRIEND IN ALL THUH WORLD!
YOU KNOW IT, CHAMP! AND TH' FEELING'S MUTUAL!
THE TRUTH REVEALED!
THE MONEY!? -PFFT!- MY REAL NAME IS PRENTISS POPVEIN, AND THIRTY YEARS AGO I WAS AS FAMOUS AS GOOFY! THE GREATEST FIGHTER CALISOTA HAD EVER SEEN...
THEN, AT THE HEAVYWEIGHT CHAMPIONSHIP, SOME JOKER TOSSED A BANANA PEEL INTO THE RING! I SLID ON IT... RIGHT INTO A KNOCKOUT PUNCH! THE LAUGHTER NEVER STOPPED! I WAS HUMILIATED...
MY CAREER WAS SHOT... AND SO WAS MY HAIR, ONCE I TORE IT OUT IN FURY! AS "TOMMY TOUPEE", I TURNED TO MANAGING... SECRETLY HOPING TO FIND A MARK ON WHOM TO TAKE MY RE-VENGE!
I HOPED TO LEAD ANOTHER MAN TO A LOSS MORE EMBARRASSING THAN MINE! GOOFY'S DEGRADATION WOULD BE MY VINDICATION... -SIGH!-
AND TO MAKE SURE HE WAS GOOD AN' RATTLED, YOU'D TURN HIS BEST FRIEND INTO FISH FOOD?! BROTHER, YOU ARE A MENTAL CASE!

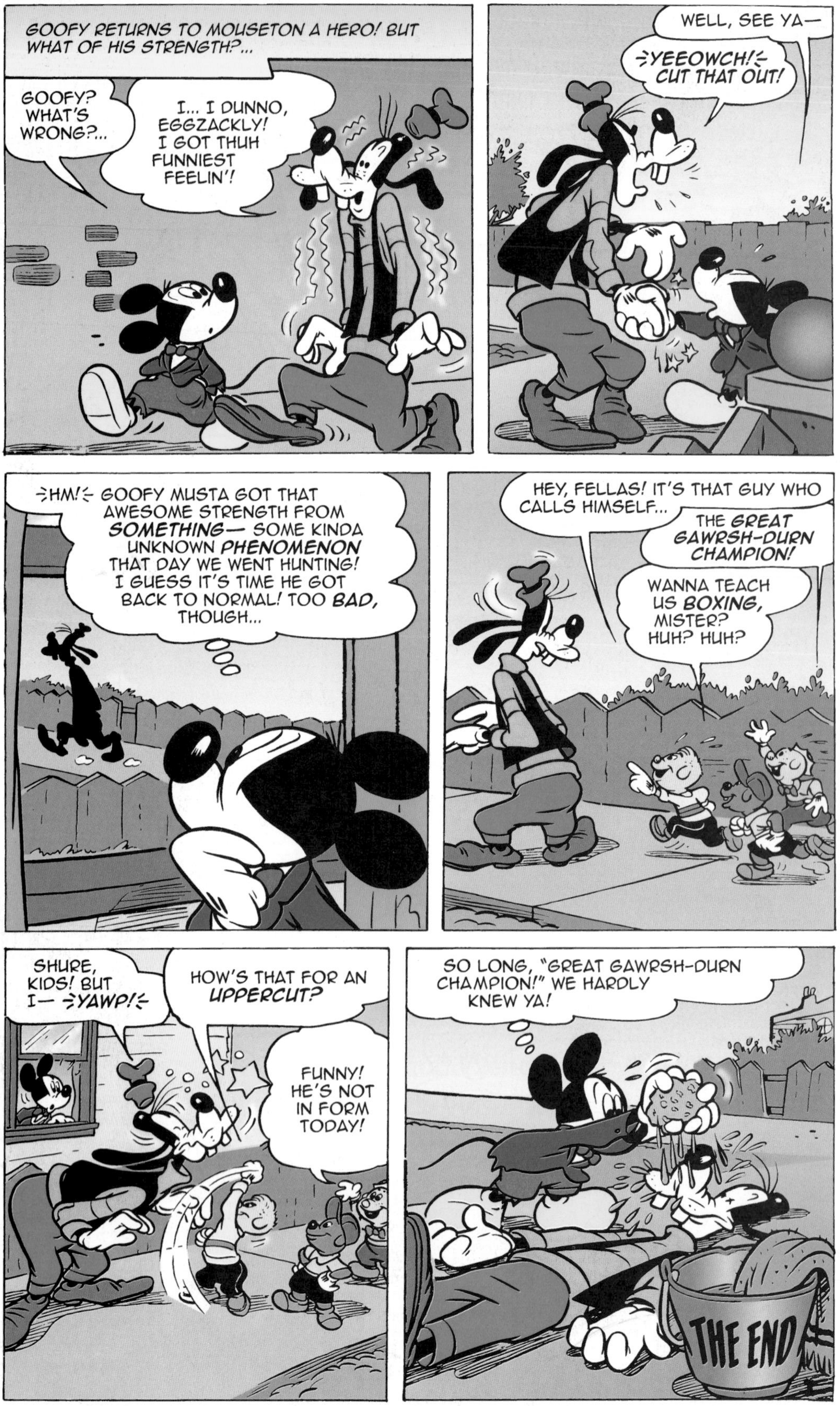
GOOFY RETURNS TO MOUSETON A HERO! BUT WHAT OF HIS STRENGTH?...
GOOFY? WHAT'S WRONG?...
I... I DUNNO, EGGZACKLY! I GOT THUH FUNNIEST FEELIN'!
WELL, SEE YA—
YEEOWCH! CUT THAT OUT!
HM! GOOFY MUSTA GOT THAT AWESOME STRENGTH FROM SOMETHING— SOME KINDA UNKNOWN PHENOMENON THAT DAY WE WENT HUNTING! I GUESS IT'S TIME HE GOT BACK TO NORMAL! TOO BAD, THOUGH...
HEY, FELLAS! IT'S THAT GUY WHO CALLS HIMSELF...
THE GREAT GAWRSH-DURN CHAMPION!
WANNA TEACH US BOXING, MISTER? HUH? HUH?
SHURE, KIDS! BUT I— YAWP!
HOW'S THAT FOR AN UPPERCUT?
FUNNY! HE'S NOT IN FORM TODAY!
SO LONG, "GREAT GAWRSH-DURN CHAMPION!" WE HARDLY KNEW YA!
THE END

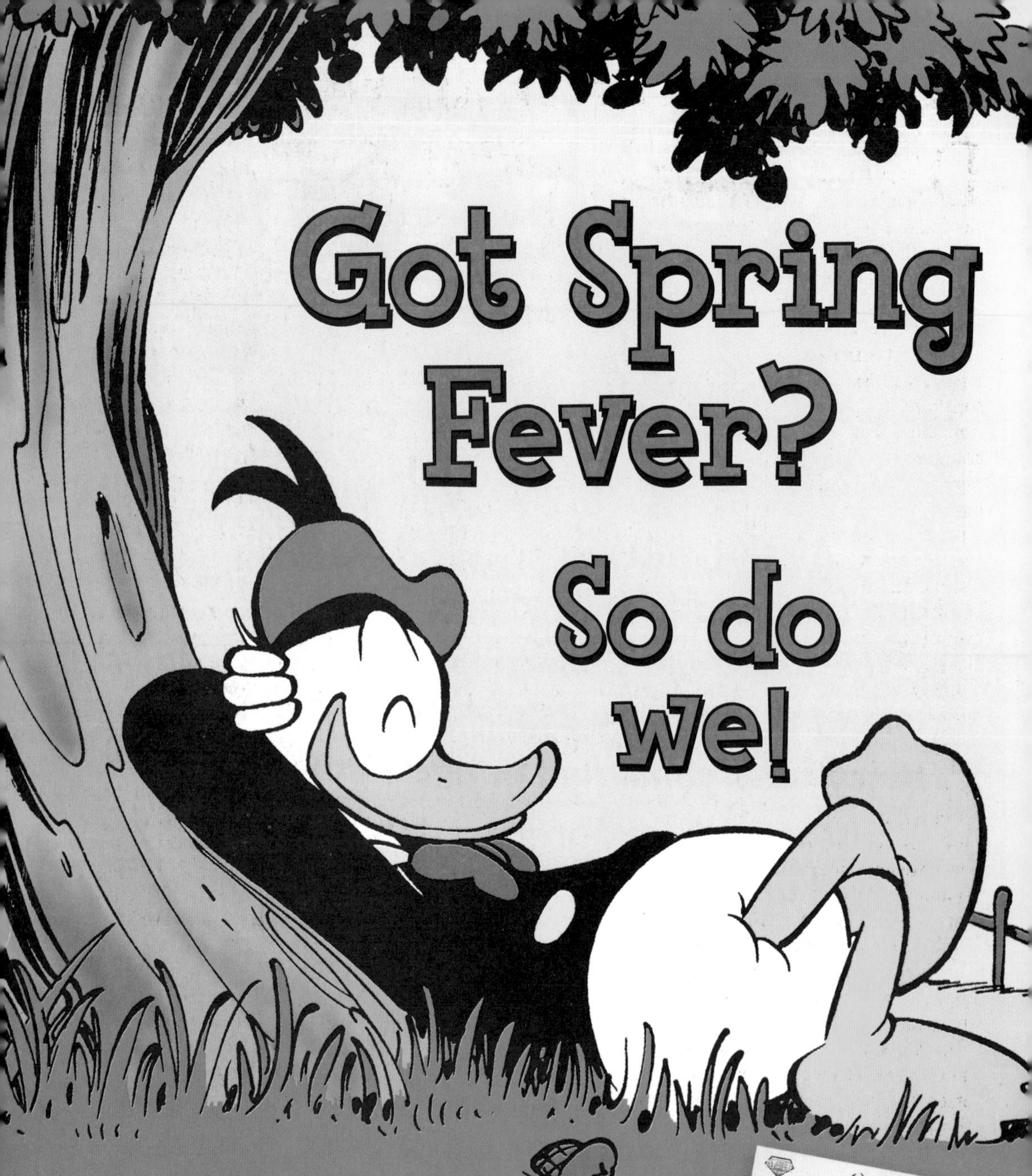
Got Spring Fever?
So do we!

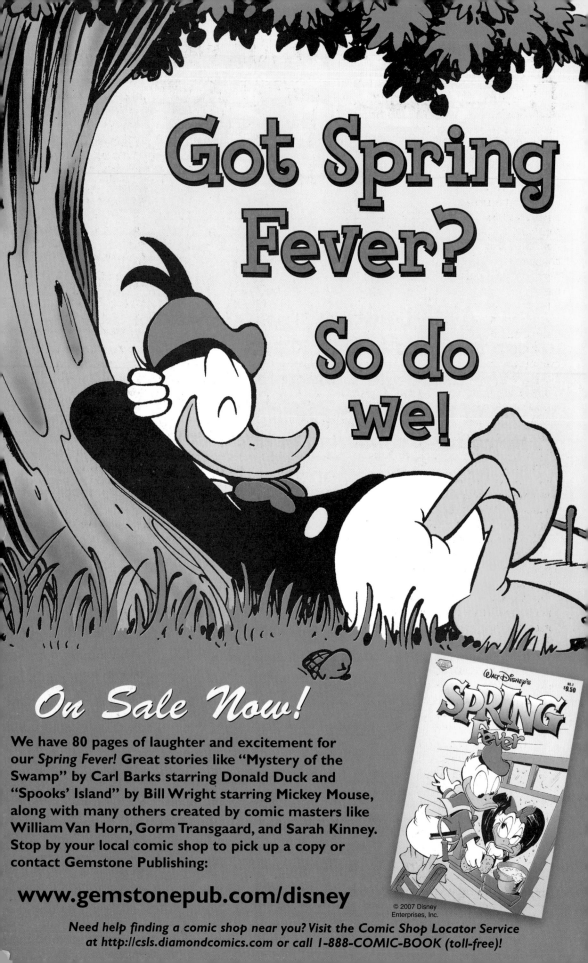